Letters from Lexington

Letters from Lexington

Reflections on Propaganda

Noam Chomsky

Common Courage Press
Monroe, Maine

AK Press
Edinburgh, Scotland

copyright ©1993 Noam Chomsky and copyright © 1990, 1991, 1992, 1993 by Sheridan Square Press, Inc., and the Institute for Media Analysis, Inc. Reprinted with permission from *Lies of Our Times;* subscriptions $24/year, US; $32/year (Canada) from *LOOT,* 145 W. 4th Street, New York, NY 10012.
All rights reserved.
Cover design by Jeff Van Peski

Common Courage Press
P.O. Box 702
Monroe, ME 04951
207-525-0900 fax: 207-525-3068

Library of Congress Cataloging in Publication Data

Chomsky, Noam
  Letters from Lexington: reflections on propaganda /
  Noam Chomsky.
    p. cm.
  Contains letters previously published in the magazine
  Lies of our times between 1990 and 1993.
    ISBN 1-56751-011-6. -- ISBN 1-56751-010-8 (pbk.)
    1. Propaganda. 2. World politics--1989- I. Lies of our
  times.
II. Title.
HM263.C446   1993
303.3'75--dc20   93-2687

British Library Cataloging in Publication Data

Chomsky, Noam
Letters from Lexington : Reflections on Propaganda
I. Title
303.375
ISBN 1-873176-06-6, paper; ISBN 1-873176-11-2, cloth

AK Press
22 Lutton Place
Edinburgh, Scotland
Eh8 9PE, Great Britain

First Printing

Contents

Introduction

The format of what follows is somewhat unusual, so perhaps a word of explanation would be in order.

When the journal of media critique *Lies of Our Times* (*LOOT*) began publishing in January 1990, I'd hoped to be able to contribute periodically, not an easy matter for me because of an extremely heavy schedule, generally extending years in advance. After two pieces (1 and 2, below), I was finding it hard to continue, amidst numerous other commitments. One element of these happens to be a huge correspondence. The reasons are many, including doubtless quirks of personality that are of no interest. But there is also a substantial reason: the genius of American democracy has been to keep people isolated from one another, lacking associations or other forms of information and interchange that might provide some (dread) substance to democratic forms; it is, incidentally, a classical insight of political theory that systems of the kind we now call "totalitarian" rely crucially on this device, which has been honed to unusual perfection in the US for a variety of historical reasons. A dissident voice that breaks through the discipline of the media on occasion commonly elicits a large response, the basic content of which is something like: "I thought I was the only person who had such thoughts—tell me more, and where I can find more." One consequence is that people tend to communicate individually, and to establish arrays of informal networks.

One of the many letters of February 1990 happened to be to my friend and co-author Edward Herman, who is the editor of *LOOT* (Feb. 11). He suggested that I might consider writing informal letters to *LOOT* now and then, in lieu of actual articles. I thought I'd try. What follows is the result, beginning with the aforementioned letter of February 11, which appears here as letter 3 (mildly edited).

Whether it was a good idea or not, others may judge.

For simplicity, I've referred to all the chapters below as "letters," though the first two technically were not. A few sources have been added, along with a bit of editing and further comments here and there. Other discrepancies that sharp-eyed *LOOT* readers may notice result from cuts for space in the original publication, or other editorial changes, there and here.

Noam Chomsky
Lexington Mass.
January 17, 1993.

1
"The Middle East Lie"

In a column entitled "The Middle East Lie," former *New York Times* Executive Editor A.M. Rosenthal, now a regular columnist, complains that "the world no longer sees the reality of the Middle East" and is thus pressuring Israel to negotiate with the PLO.[1] This "blunder" would lead to "another Palestinian state" in addition to "the existing Palestinian state of Jordan," and inevitable war. The problem is that "the world" is in thrall to "a fundamental historical distortion": "the lie [that] Israel refuses to negotiate for peace." "The truth" is that Israel has been trying for 40 years to negotiate a peaceful settlement with its neighbors, while the Arab answer has been "rejection and war." The sole exception is Egyptian President Sadat's trip to Jerusalem in 1977 and the Camp David treaty that followed. "The road to peace is through direct talks between Israel and her Arab neighbors"—crucially excluding the Palestinians.

Rosenthal's tale is indeed "the truth" as constructed by Israel and the United States—and faithfully recounted for many years by the *New York Times,* under his leadership and since. But the truth is rather different.

Consider first the period since the Israeli conquests of June 1967. The record for the first decade, under the rule of the "pragmatic" and "moderate" Labor Party, is documented from cabinet records by Labor Party functionary Yossi Beilin.[2] The guiding principle throughout, as outlined by Haim Herzog, now President of Israel, was that the indigenous population cannot be "participants in any way in a land that has been consecrated to our people for thousands of years. To the Jews of this land there cannot be any partner." Accordingly, independent political activities were barred, as when Prime Minister Golda Meir, in 1972, for-

3

bade a pro-Jordanian political conference in the West Bank. The governing Likud coalition has been still more extreme. Its central component, Herut, the party of Menachem Begin and Yitzhak Shamir, officially and publicly refuses to renounce Israel's claim to Jordan.

On June 19, 1967, the Israeli cabinet voted 11-10 to transmit an offer via the US for a settlement with Syria and Egypt on the international (pre-June 1967) borders, but with Israel keeping Gaza and no mention of Jordan and the West Bank. This proposal, which Abba Eban described as "the most dramatic initiative that the government of Israel ever took before or since," was rescinded a year later, when Israel put forth the Allon Plan, called "territorial compromise" for cosmetic purposes. Its terms were that Israel was to keep the Syrian Golan Heights, the Gaza Strip, Eastern Sinai, and whatever it found of value in the West Bank, including about 40 percent of the land, but not the bulk of the population, for whom Israel would take no responsibility; they would be stateless or under Jordanian administration. This has remained the Labor Party position in essentials, with various tactical modifications in response to changing contingencies.

No further Israeli initiatives are known, and Israel has forcefully rejected other proposals. The sole exception is the Camp David arrangements, which were accepted by Begin's ruling Likud coalition over the objections of major elements of the Labor leadership, who opposed the required withdrawal from settlements Labor had established in the Egyptian Sinai. Despite this feature, the Camp David settlement was considered advantageous by Israeli hawks because it removed the major Arab deterrent (Egypt) from the conflict, with predictable effects: allowing Israel to attack its northern neighbor and to integrate the occupied territories. As observed in retrospect by Israeli strategic analyst Avner Yaniv, the result of Camp David was that "Israel would be free to sustain military operations against the PLO in Lebanon as well as settlement activity on the West

Bank."[3] A vast increase in US aid from 1978 ensured that these would be exactly the consequences of what Rosenthal calls "the political and spiritual triumph of Camp David."

Turning to the Arab record, the first major Arab peace initiative long preceded Sadat's trip to Jerusalem in 1977, contrary to the conventional fantasy Rosenthal recounts. It was in February 1971, when President Sadat accepted UN mediator Gunnar Jarring's proposal for a full peace treaty on the international borders, offering nothing to the Palestinians. This proposal, which conformed closely to the official US stand, was recognized by Israel to be a genuine peace offer, but rejected. Israel was backed by the US, which preferred "stalemate," as later explained by Henry Kissinger, who managed to wrest control of Middle East policy from his hated rival, Secretary of State William Rogers, in time to beat back the threat of a diplomatic settlement.

Another major Arab initiative was in January 1976, when Syria, Jordan and Egypt backed a UN Security Council resolution calling for a two-state settlement on the international borders with "appropriate arrangements...to guarantee...the sovereignty, territorial integrity and political independence of all states in the area and their right to live in peace within secure and recognized boundaries." This is the crucial wording of UN 242, which the US government and the *Times* claim to regard as the basis for any settlement—though (along with Israel) they insist upon an interpretation of UN 242 that departs in essential ways from the international consensus, to which the US too adhered pre-1971. The Security Council resolution was openly backed by the PLO, which actually "prepared" it according to Haim Herzog, then Israel's UN Ambassador.

Israel refused to attend the UN session. The Labor government announced that it would not negotiate with any Palestinians on any political issue and would not negotiate with the PLO under any circumstances. In apparent retaliation against the UN, Israeli jets bombed and strafed Palestinian refugee camps and nearby villages, killing dozens of people in what it called a preventive strike, an act that elicited little comment here. The US vetoed the Security Council resolution, as it did again in 1980, thus rendering the UN largely irrelevant.

There are numerous other examples, including offers by Yasser Arafat for negotiations with Israel leading to mutual recognition in the mid-1980s. All of this has been excised from official history, apart from Sadat's 1977 moves, which, though less acceptable to Israel than his 1971 offer, did lead to a US-Israeli response. The reason is that after the surprising Arab successes in the October 1973 war, it was understood—even by Kissinger—that Egypt could not be simply ignored so that it was necessary to move to a fallback position: removing Egypt from the conflict, a policy initiated by Kissinger and consummated at Camp David, with the consequences noted.

Times history follows the official line throughout. In its news reports and commentary, the major Arab initiatives are down the memory hole, apart from that of Sadat in 1977—which is admitted into "history" because it could be molded by Washington into an arrangement that satisfied US-Israeli needs. The "peace process" is defined as whatever the US proposes: blocking the peace process for 20 years, in the present case. The *Times* regularly refused to report Arafat's offers; even letters referring to them were banned. The contributions of Jerusalem correspondent Thomas Friedman were a particularly noteworthy contribution to this remarkable record of historical engineering in the service of power.[4]

Turning back to the earlier years, from 1948 to 1967 the truth is also rather more complex than Rosenthal's "truth," including initiatives from Syria, Jordan, and Egypt that were rebuffed, and aggressive Israeli actions that undermined steps towards peace. To cite only one case, after a coup in 1949 apparently backed by the CIA, Syrian leader Husni Zaim "made a determined effort to come to terms with Israel," even offering "to settle 300,000 Palestinian refugees, nearly half the total number, in Syria." Prime Minister David Ben-Gurion refused even to meet with him, and no serious attention was given to his offer.[5]

In summary, while Rosenthal's "truth" is faithful to the *Times* version, it bears only incidental resemblance to the truth.

As for Rosenthal's "existing Palestinian state," it is true that Jordan is so designated by both major Israeli political groupings. For Rosenthal, that suffices, and it is irrelevant that Jordan and the Palestinians vigorously reject this characterization; what right do mere Arabs have to express their views about their homes when the interests of Rosenthal's favorites are at stake? We might ask how the *Times* would react to an Arab claim that the Jews do not merit a "second homeland" because they already have New York, with a huge Jewish population, Jewish-run media, a Jewish mayor, and domination of cultural and economic life. We learn a good deal about the Newspaper of Record— and the intellectual culture that accepts all this without a murmur—from consideration of this question.

LOOT, 1.1, January 1990

Notes

1. *New York Times,* March 21, 1989.
2. *Mehiro shel Ihud* (Revivim, 1985).
3. Yaniv, *Dilemmas of Security* (Oxford, 1987), 70.
4. See my *Necessary Illusions* (South End, 1989), particularly 290-95. For further background and a record as the process developed, see my *Peace in the Middle East?* (Pantheon, 1974); *Towards a New Cold War* (Pantheon, 1982); *Fateful Triangle* (South End, 1983); *Pirates & Emperors* (Claremont, 1986; Amana, 1988); *Deterring Democracy,* "Afterword" (Hill & Wang, 1992, extended edition).
5. Avi Shlaim, *Collusion Across the Jordan* (Columbia, 1988), 428; Tom Segev, *1949: the First Israelis* (Free Press, 1986), 16. See now also Itamar Rabinovich, *The Road not Taken* (Oxford, 1991).

2
Defensive Aggression

When a state carries out aggression, its propaganda system has the responsibility to justify the act and suppress the reasons for it in favor of acceptable pretexts. The US invasion of Panama in December fits the script to perfection.

The invasion posed some novel tasks. Earlier resort to state violence could routinely be justified by appeal to the Soviet threat, but that device has lost any shred of credibility. Something new was needed, and fortunately, the foundation had been laid, notably by the well-timed orchestration of hysteria over Latin American narcotraffickers ("the drug war") two months earlier. Americans hate Noriega, the media correctly relate, so he must go. Why did Americans hate Noriega in 1989, but not in 1985? Why is it necessary to overthrow him now but not then? These are the obvious and fundamental questions. They were systematically evaded. State policy was thus effectively shielded from scrutiny.

Noriega had long been a willing and useful ally, but by 1985, the US began to reassess his role and within two years had decided to remove him. A program of economic warfare was designed to erode Noriega's support among the poor and black population, while minimizing the impact on the US business community, a GAO official testified before Congress.[1] As policy shifted, the media followed suit in the classic pattern, demonizing Noriega, whipping up popular frenzy over a fraudulent "drug war," and preparing the ground for the invasion.

In the post-1985 media campaign, Noriega was presented as a demon who must be exorcised, a repeat of the Qaddafi project from 1981, when the Reagan Administra-

9

tion selected him as a convenient punching bag, available when needed to whip up fear and jingoist sentiment among the domestic public. Is Noriega's gangsterism and corruption the reason for his fall from grace, or even a factor? The question is easily answered. Noriega was known to be a thug when he was a US ally, and remained so, with no relevant change, as the government (hence the media) turned against him. Furthermore, he does not approach the criminality of people the US cheerfully supports. The 1988 Americas Watch report on *Human Rights in Panama* details abuses, but nothing remotely comparable to the record of US clients in the region, or elsewhere. One finds next to nothing about these crucial matters in the chauvinist media blitz.

The real reasons are not hard to discern. One black mark against Noriega in 1985 was his support for the Central American (Contadora) peace process. His commitment to the US war against Nicaragua was in question, and when the Iran-contra affair broke, his usefulness was clearly at an end. A more general problem was his nationalist and populist gestures, a carryover from the Torrijos period, when the traditional oligarchy was displaced. Yet another problem was noted by the London *Economist*: on New Year's Day 1990, "the United States has to hand over to Panama the preponderant share of control over the Panama Canal and the military bases around it"; and a few years later the rest follows. A major oil pipeline is 60 percent owned by Panama. Clearly, traditional and more reliable US clients had to be restored to power, and there was not much time to spare.[2]

The Bush Administration, helpfully, took pains to make it clear that Noriega's crimes were not a factor in the invasion. As the troops landed in Panama, the White House announced new high technology sales to China, noting that $300 million in business for US firms was at stake and that contacts had secretly resumed a few weeks after the Tiananmen Square massacre. Washington also barred entry to two

Chinese scholars invited by US universities, in deference to the Chinese authorities. It also announced new subsidized agricultural sales to China and a plan to lift a ban on loans to Iraq. In comparison to Bush's friends in Beijing and Baghdad, Noriega looks positively benign.[3]

Some sensed a "lack of political and moral consistency" in the action against Noriega just as Washington "kisses the hands of the Chinese dictators" (A.M. Rosenthal).[4] The apparent inconsistency vanishes as soon as doctrinal constraints are put aside. In all cases, the actions serve the needs of US power and privilege. The media succeeded in overlooking these not-too-subtle points—and even many of the facts (notably, the gesture of friendship to Saddam Hussein).

Another pretext for the invasion was our commitment to democracy, so profound that we simply could not stand by in silence when Noriega stole the 1989 election that had been won by the US-backed candidate, Guillermo Endara, now placed in office by the invasion. There is an obvious way to test this thesis: What happened in the preceding election in 1984, when Noriega was still *our* thug? The answer is that Noriega stole the election with more violence than in 1989, barring the victory of Arnulfo Arias and installing Nicolas Ardito Barletta, since known as "fraudito" in Panama. Washington opposed Arias, who was considered an independent nationalist, preferring Barletta, whose campaign was financed with US government funds through the National Endowment for Democracy, according to US Ambassador Everett Briggs. George Shultz was sent down to legitimate the fraud, praising "Panamanian democracy" at the inauguration. The media carefully looked the other way.

Our 1989 favorite, Guillermo Endara, was close to Arias and remained his spokesman in Panama until his death in 1988 in self-imposed exile. The *Washington Post* now reports that Endara was chosen to run in 1989 "largely because of his close ties to the late legendary Panamanian politician Arnulfo Arias, who was ousted from the presidency by the military three times since the 1940s"; the account of Arias's fate is accurate, but a trifle selective. The media once again looked the other way when, during the 1989 invasion, Endara denounced the "fraud of 1984"; and they do not ask why our fabled "yearning for democracy" was mysteriously awakened only when Noriega had become a nuisance to Washington rather than an asset.[5]

Another pretext was that Noriega was a drug dealer—as was known long before, while he was on the CIA payroll. Furthermore, he was not alone. Shortly after Noriega stole the 1984 elections with Washington's applause, the US Attorney in Miami identified Panamanian banks as a major conduit for drug money. A year earlier, a Senate report on banking had described Panama as a major center of criminal capital, and a key link in drug transshipment and drug money laundering. The US invasion returned the bankers to power in Panama. It all makes good sense. As Drug Czar in the early 1980s, George Bush cancelled the small federal program aimed at banks engaged in laundering drug money, and this central link in the trade has been excluded from the current "drug war." Ghetto kids who sell crack arouse our ire, but not the civilized folk in the plush offices.[6]

The immediate pretext for the invasion was to "protect American lives." There had been "literally hundreds of cases of harassment and abuse of Americans" in recent months by Noriega's forces, White House spokesman Marlin Fitzwater announced—though, curiously, no warning to Americans to stay away, up until the day of the invasion. A US soldier was killed under disputed circumstances, but what tipped the scales was the threat to the wife of an officer who was arrested and beaten. Bush "often has difficulty in emotionally charged situations," the *New York Times* reported, "but his deep feelings clearly came through" when he spoke of this incident, proclaiming, in his best Ollie North rendition, that "this President" is not going to stand by while American womanhood is threatened.[7]

The press did not explain why "this President" refused even to issue a protest when, a few weeks earlier, an American nun, Diana Ortiz, had been kidnapped, tortured, and sexually abused by the Guatemalan police—or why the story was not worth reporting when it appeared on the wires on November 6. Nor were Bush's "deep feelings" contrasted with the response of "this president" to the treatment of American women and other religious and humanitarian workers in El Salvador a few weeks later, a small footnote to the brutal government actions praised by Secretary of State James Baker at a November 29 press conference as "absolutely appropriate"—a comment that largely escaped notice, perhaps regarded as not too useful right after the murder of the Jesuit intellectuals.[8]

Government-media doctrine holds that Bush "had few alternatives" to invasion, having failed to oust Noriega by other means (R.W. Apple). "Mr. Bush may have seen no alternative to invasion," Tom Wicker added, though as a dove, he regards Bush's arguments as not "conclusive."[9] The underlying assumption is that the US naturally has every right to achieve its aims, whatever they may be, so that violence is legitimate if peaceful means fail. The principle has broad application. It could readily be invoked by the terrorists who destroyed Pan Am 103, an act bitterly denounced on its first anniversary just as the US invaded Panama. They too could plead that they had exhausted peaceful means. But the doctrine has another crucial feature: the right to violence is reserved to the United States.

This doctrine may be tacitly invoked, as in the present case. But it cannot be explicitly asserted, because it reveals far too much.

The fundamental doctrine is further clarified by the attitude towards international law. That its precepts were violated by the invasion was sometimes noted, but dismissed, on the grounds that the "legalities are murky"[10] (which is nonsense) or simply an irrelevance (which is correct; the toughest guy on the block need not play by the

rules). Exactly ten years earlier, Vietnam invaded Cambodia after barbaric attacks against Vietnamese villages with
thousands of casualties, overthrowing the Pol Pot regime.
By any standards of reason or moral concern, the justification for this invasion is far more plausible than anything
that Washington could offer regarding Panama. But in that
case, the legalities were neither murky nor irrelevant.
Rather, Vietnam's violation of international law deeply of-
fended our tender sensibilities, establishing Vietnam as "the
Prussians of Southeast Asia" (*New York Times*) whom we
must punish, along with the people of Cambodia, by economic warfare and tacit support for the Khmer Rouge.

The radically different reactions are readily explained
by the doctrine that the US alone enjoys the right of lawless
violence. But the obvious questions remain unasked, and
the insights effectively suppressed.

Only a step away, the veil lifts and elementary truths
are readily perceived. Israel's leading military analyst,
Ze'ev Schiff, comments that there is nothing remarkable
about the US invasion of Panama, "neither from a military
standpoint—in that the American forces are killing innocent Panamanian civilians... nor from a political standpoint, when a great power employs its military forces
against a small neighbor, with pretexts that Washington
would dismiss at once if they were offered by other states."
Like the bombing of Libya and other military operations,
this one reveals "that Washington permits itself what other
powers, including the USSR, do not permit themselves,
though they plainly have no less justification."[11]

This is a mere sample, but enough to illustrate "the
kind of hard-hitting, no holds barred reporting that makes
the press such an essential component of this country's
democratic system," as Sanford Ungar writes, overcome
with awe at the magnificence of his profession.[12]

Notes

1. Paul Blustein and Steven Mufson, *Washington Post Weekly,* Dec. 25, 1989. For further details, here and below, see *Deterring Democracy,* chaps. 4 (on the "drug war") and 5 (on Panama).

2. *Economist,* Dec. 23; Martha Hamilton, *WP Weekly,* Dec. 25, 1989.

3. Andrew Rosenthal, *NYT,* Dec. 20; Maureen Dowd, *NYT,* Dec. 19; Anthony Flint, *Boston Globe,* Dec. 21; AP, Dec. 20, Dec. 22, 1989.

4. *NYT,* Dec. 22, 1989.

5. Julia Preston, *WP weekly,* Dec. 25, 1989. AP, Dec. 20; *BG,* Dec. 21, 1989. On the 1984 elections, see Seymour Hersh, *NYT,* June 22, 1986; John Weeks, "Panama: The roots of current political instability," *Third World Quarterly,* July 1987; Alfonso Chardy, *Miami Herald,* March 3, 1988; Ken Silverstein, *Columbia Journalism Review,* May/June 1988. On our "yearning for democracy," see letter 6.

6. INFORPRESS (*Central America Report,* Guatemala City), vol. XI, no. 31, 1984, citing *Miami Herald.* Staff Study, "Crime and Secrecy: The Use of Offshore Banks and Companies," Permanent Subcommittee on Investigations of the Committee on Governmental Affairs, U.S. Senate, 1983. On the predictable consequences of returning the drug ring to power, see my *Year 501* (South End, 1993), chap. 3.4.

7. *BG,* Dec. 20; Andrew Rosenthal, *NYT,* Dec. 22, 1989.

8. AP, Nov. 6, 29, 1989.

9. *NYT,* Dec. 21, 22, 1989.

10. *Wall Street Journal,* Dec. 26.

11. *Ha'aretz,* Dec. 21, 1989.

12. *Foreign Policy,* Winter 1989/90.

3
The *Sunday Times* Makes for a Day of No Rest

February 11, 1990

Dear *LOOT*,

I guess a sign of my improving health is that the *Times* infuriates me as much as it always did (over the summer, when I was ill, it only made me laugh). So take today. I'm enclosing three items that might be of interest to *LOOT*— though they involve not so much lies, literally, as cowardice and dishonesty.

The first is an article on Timor, entitled "East Timor Bishop Writes of Torture." In the conventional style, it carefully excludes the role of the US government and its Newspaper of Record, although both played an important role in what the author euphemistically calls the "forced annexation." There's not a phrase on the character of that "annexation." By contrast, no article on the Khmer Rouge appears without some appropriate descriptive phrase ("the KR, who killed millions of Cambodians," etc.), just to make sure that the reader knows we're talking about evil Communists.

The article by Steven Erlanger, "Southeast Asia is Now No. 1 Source of U.S. Heroin," also has a few interesting omissions. First, while Erlanger mentions that for the past 25 years the US has been struggling to deal with the drug flow from Southeast Asia, he doesn't add the minor point that the problem arose because the CIA entered the game at that time to organize and amplify the relatively small drug racket (itself largely in the hands of US-supported Kuomintang gangsters in Burma). So, having nurtured the monster as part of its "clandestine war" in Laos, the US has been struggling to tame its creature—all unmentioned. (Also unmentioned in the same connection is that Afghanistan's recent emergence as a major drug source has similar causes, and that, more generally, the trail of clandestine operations and of drugs intertwine in ways that are more than coincidental since shortly after World War II).[1]

A second interesting omission has to do with Thailand. Erlanger describes how US diplomats are trying to get across to the Thais the error of their ways in failing to stop the export of heroin to the US. The diplomats don't, of course, accuse Thailand of actively exporting drugs and using what methods it can to ram them down the throats of American consumers, putting the screws on Washington so that it cannot act to stem the flow, spending massive amounts of money advertising to encourage drug use and to open new markets (women and youth, particularly). But that is exactly what the US is doing in Thailand with the highly profitable lethal drug manufactured here: tobacco, a far greater killer than heroin—indeed, than all hard drugs combined. Right in the midst of the government-media furor about the "drug war" in September 1989, the US Trade Representative considered a tobacco company demand that Washington impose trade sanctions on Thailand because it was trying to regulate tobacco, restricting imports and advertising (the US had already forced Japan and South Korea to import its lethal drugs by the same device). Surgeon-General Koop and others testified that this was a replay of the Opium Wars, an indescribable scandal, etc. The press kept silent; no memories of these events trouble the *Times*, or the earnest diplomats it chooses to quote today.

Another example is the Mark Uhlig article on Nicaraguan elections: "For the Sandinista Faithful, an Item to Fit Every Mood." Uhlig is properly derisive about the infamous Sandinistas, who are handing out T-shirts to influence voters and in other such ways demonstrating that they are totalitarian maniacs. Obviously, nothing like that could ever happen in a civilized country, surely not the world's leading democracy. This is standard reporting these days.

That's page 28. On p. 30, there is an article about how Lyndon Johnson stole the senatorial elections in Texas, a crucial stepping-stone to the White House. The *New Yorker* recently ran a series on LBJ's early career, which makes the Sandinistas look like idealized Jeffersonians in comparison. There are also a few questions about the dawn of Camelot, as some may recall, not to speak of other cases. Fortunately, we are immune from cognitive dissonance. If anyone had been so crude as to compare pages 28 and 30, the response would have surely been that the LBJ fraud was long ago, only 170 years after the American revolution, so it is unfair to bring it up—we hadn't quite got our act together.

Apologies for the tirade. I had to get rid of some anger before settling down to work.

Sincerely,

Noam

LOOT, 1.3, March 1990

Notes

1. See, among other sources, Alfred McCoy, et al., *The Politics of Heroin in Southeast Asia* (Harper & Row, 1972); Henrik Kruger, *The Great Heroin Coup* (South End, 1980).

4
Notes on
the Culture of Democracy

March 18, 1990

Dear *LOOT*,

A few reflections on media coverage of the Nicaraguan election, which provides much insight into the dominant political culture.

The most striking feature was the demand for unanimity. A *Times* headline reads: "Americans United in Joy But Divided Over Policy" (Elaine Sciolino).[1] The "policy division" has to do with who gets credit for the joyous outcome. Such phrases as "United in Joy" are not entirely without precedent; one might find them, perhaps, in North Korean or Albanian propaganda. Obviously the issue was contentious, at least to Nicaraguans. But not to American elites, who are quite happy to depict themselves as dedicated totalitarians.

The first two-thirds of Sciolino's review of the Unity in Joy samples the reactions of contra supporters: Elliott Abrams, Jeane Kirkpatrick, Fred Iklé, Oliver North, Robert Leiken, Ronald Reagan. It then proceeds: "On the other side, Lawrence Pezullo, who was appointed Ambassador to Nicaragua by President Carter, called the election results 'fantastic'." Fortunately, the tradition of balanced reporting is preserved, with the whole broad spectrum of conceivable opinion amply represented.

Pezullo's achievements "on the other side" are not described, so let us recall a few highlights of his career as a left-wing extremist, balancing "the first side." Appointed when Carter's support for Somoza was becoming difficult to sustain, Pezullo took the lead in advocating the bombing of civilian areas at a time when tens of thousands were being murdered by the US-backed National Guard, and oversaw the efforts to guarantee their rule after Somoza had to be abandoned. When these too failed, he took part in the fall-back efforts: ferrying Guard officers out of the country in planes with Red Cross markings (a war crime, if anyone cares), initiation of CIA subversion, and an "aid" program designed largely to pay off international banks and strengthen opponents of the Sandinistas in the governing coalition—what is commonly described in US media fare as proof of Washington's benign intent towards the Sandinistas before they revealed their true colors.

After reviewing a few similar representatives of "the other side," Sciolino's report ends with the observation that some opponents of contra aid "were not entirely comfortable with the results," citing Lawrence Birns of the Council on Hemispheric Affairs, who "seemed to side with the Sandinistas," expressing his "inner rage that the corner bully won over the little guy."

So there are "two sides," which differed on how to eliminate the Sandinistas in favor of US clients and are now "United in Joy." And there is one person who "*seems* to side with the Sandinistas"—but couldn't *really* be that far out of step.

Sciolino notes incidentally that "Sandinista supporters expressed sadness." Since Americans were "United in Joy," it follows, by simple logic, that these odd creatures are not Americans, or perhaps not people. Other *Times* reporting suggests the latter interpretation. Thus, when Clyde Farnsworth reported that "no one is arguing strenuously that [the embargo] be amended," many featherless bipeds were arguing strenuously that these murderous and illegal measures be terminated, a deviation that evidently renders them inadmissible to the human species.[2]

As amply documented elsewhere, such unanimity has been characteristic of the Free Press, with some tactical division about how to restore Nicaragua to the "Central America mode" of El Salvador and Guatemala, as the liberal press formulated the task at hand. Sometimes one finds a bit of noise in the system; in the case of the elections, scarcely even that.

Pre-election coverage was overwhelmingly anti-Sandinista. UNO was the "democratic opposition," on the sole grounds that the coalition had been forged by Washington and included the major business interests; further democratic credentials being unnecessary, they remained unreported. Commentary and reporting on the Sandinistas was harsh and derisive. The "ultraliberal" *Boston Globe* did break ranks by running an Op-Ed by Daniel Ortega—with an accompanying caricature of an ominous thug in a Soviet field marshal's uniform wearing designer glasses, in case readers might be momentarily misled.[3] Media monitors have yet to come up with a single phrase suggesting that an FSLN victory might be preferable for Nicaragua. Even journalists and Op-Ed contributors who privately felt that way did not say it; not out of fear, I suppose, but because they took for granted that such an idea would be unintelligible, a statement without cognitive meaning, on a par with "the US is a leading terrorist state," or "Washington is blocking the peace process," or other departures from dogma (even truisms such as these). In a Free Society, *all* must march on command, or keep silent. There must have been some departures somewhere, but the general performance would have impressed many a dictator.

On TV, Peter Jennings opened the international news by announcing that Nicaragua is going to have its "first free election in a decade.'"[4] Three crucial "facts" are presupposed: (1) the elections under Somoza were free; (2) there was no free election in 1984; (3) the 1990 election was free and uncoerced. A standard footnote to (2) is that Ortega was driven to accept the 1990 elections by US pressure; here opinion divides in the usual way, with "conservatives" and "liberals" bickering over who gains credit for the achievement.

Out of charity, we may put aside point (1), though not without noting that it has been a staple of the liberal media, with their frequent reference to "restoring democracy" in Nicaragua. The second point expresses a fundamental dogma, which brooks no deviation and is immune to fact; I need not review the actual facts, familiar to those who have been able to—or chose to—escape the reigning doctrinal system.[5] The footnote ignores the unacceptable (hence unreportable) fact that the next election had always been scheduled for 1990, and that the total effect of US machinations was to advance it by a few months.

The most interesting point, however, is the third. Suppose that the USSR were to follow the US model as the Baltic states declare independence, organizing a proxy army to attack them under orders to hit "soft targets" so as to cause maximal harm to civilians, demolishing the economy through economic warfare, and so on, in the familiar routine; and then, when elections come, telling the population, loud and clear, that they can vote for the CP or be murdered and starve. Perhaps some unreconstructed Stalinist might call this a "free and fair election." Surely no one else would.

Or suppose that the Arab states were to reduce Israel to the level of Ethiopia, then issuing a credible threat that they would drive it the rest of the way unless it "cried uncle" and voted for their candidate. Someone who called this a "democratic election," "free and fair," would be dismissed as an outright Nazi, quite rightly.

Those familiar with the basic facts will have no difficulty recognizing the pertinence of the analogy. It follows that anyone who called these elections "free and fair" was not merely a totalitarian, but of a rather special variety. The description holds of virtually everyone; in fact, I have found exactly *one* commentator in the mainstream to whom it does not apply.

It was obvious from the outset that the US would never tolerate free and fair elections. The point was underscored by repeated announcements that the terror and economic war would continue unless a "free choice" met the conditions of the Enforcer. It was made official as the electoral campaign opened in early November 1989, when the White House announced that the embargo, which had already caused $3 billion worth of damage according to UNO economist Francisco Mayorga, would continue unless the population followed US orders. Any intelligent 10-year-old would understand at once that your choice is not "free and fair" when you have a gun pointed at your head. In an intellectual culture that is more free and independent, as in the military-run terror state of Guatemala, the media had no difficulty perceiving these trivialities.[6]

To be sure, the kinds of "divisions" that are allowed to make it to the *Times* were to be found on this issue as well. There were, in the first place, a few who simply denied that the military and economic wars were having any notable impact. Turning to those who at least pretended to be serious, we find the usual two categories. The "conservatives" didn't mention these crucial factors, and hailed the stunning triumph of democracy. The "liberals" did mention them, and then hailed the stunning triumph of democracy. As always, the second category play a far more significant role within the indoctrination system, since they set the outer limits of tolerable dissent.

A few examples.[7]

New Republic editor Michael Kinsley recalled an earlier article of his, omitting its crucial content: that terrorist attacks against civilian targets are legitimate if a "cost-benefit analysis" shows that the "blood and misery" yields consequences that he takes to be favorable. Kinsley then observes that "impoverishing the people of Nicaragua was precisely the point of the contra war and the parallel" economic warfare, and it is "Orwellian" to blame the Sandinistas "for wrecking the economy while devoting our best efforts to doing precisely that." "It was also Orwellian for the United States, having created the disaster [that was UNO's "best election issue"], to be posturing as the exhorter and arbiter of free elections." He then proceeds to posture precisely in that Orwellian style, hailing the "free election" and "triumph of democracy."[8]

In another illustration of the liberal mode, Anthony Lewis of the *New York Times* tells us that "the Reagan policy produced only misery, death and shame"—including the methods of strangling Nicaragua preferred by the liberals, a fact unmentioned. He then moves on to impressive rhetorical flourishes about the success of Nicaragua's "experiment in peace and democracy" in this "romantic age," and the triumph of "Jefferson's idea: government with the consent of the governed." He even descends to citing Vaclav Havel, who endeared himself to the intellectual community by declaring, Pat Robertson-style, that America has been the "defender of freedom," as the happy folk in Central America can attest, along with a few others who might reach consciousness.[9]

At the dissident extreme, William LeoGrande also hailed the promise of the "democratic elections in Nicaragua," while noting that "In the name of democracy, Washington put excruciating military and economic pressure on Nicaragua in order to force the Sandinistas out of power." Now, he continues, "the United States must show that its commitment to democracy in Central America extends to pressuring friendly conservative governments as well." Thus, having demonstrated its "commitment to democracy" by terror and economic warfare, the US should "extend" this libertarian fervor to its friends as well.[10]

Turning to the shining light of American liberalism, the lead editorial in the *Boston Globe* was headlined "Rallying to Chamorro."[11] All those who truly "love Nicaraguans," editor Martin Nolan declared, "must now rally to Chamorro." Suppose that in 1964 someone had written that all Goldwater supporters "must now rally to Johnson." Such a person would, again, have been regarded as a throwback to the days when the Gauleiters and Commissars recognized that everyone must rally behind der Führer. The conception of democracy that is upheld towards the extremes of Kennedy liberalism is most enlightening.

Nolan goes on to explain that "Ortega was not an adept politician. His beloved masses could not eat slogans and voted with their stomachs, not their hearts." If Ortega had been more adept, he could have provided them with food—by following Nolan's advice and capitulating to the master. Now, in this "blessing of democracy," "at long last, Nicaragua itself has spoken"—freely, and without duress.

While Nolan's vulgarity may be a bit extreme, the general picture scarcely departs from these examples, taken from the liberal fringe. I'll stop here, with a summary comment.

Three features of the election coverage are particularly striking: first, the extraordinary uniformity, which could scarcely be matched in a well-run totalitarian state; second, the hatred and contempt for democracy revealed with such stark clarity across the political spectrum; third, and most revealing of all, the utter incapacity to perceive these simple facts. Exceptions are so marginal as to be counted mere statistical error. The facts merit careful thought. They tell us a great deal about the political culture, and give a revealing insight into the dedicated assault on democracy that has been such a dramatic feature of the period that the Commissar class, quite predictably, describes as "the triumph of democracy."

Perhaps there should be little here to surprise those who have been following the performance of the Free Press and the intellectual community it samples and addresses, including the "establishment left," to borrow the phrase of editor Charles William Maynes of *Foreign Policy*, the liberal alternative to *Foreign Affairs*, in his ode to the American crusade "to spread the cause of democracy."[12] The phrase "establishment left" refers to the *New York Times*. A proper requiem for the dominant political culture.

Sincerely,

Noam

Notes

1. *NYT,* Feb. 27, 1990.
2. *NYT,* Nov. 10, 1985. See letter 13 for another illustration of the conditions for entry into the species.
3. *BG,* Eeb. 22, 1990.
4. ABC TV news, Feb. 20, 1990, 7 PM.
5. For review of the reaction to Nicaragua's 1984 election outside the US Free Press, and comparison of its reporting of this election with those at the same time in nearby US terror states, see Edward S. Herman and N. Chomsky, *Manufacturing Consent* (Pantheon, 1988), chap. 3.
6. See *Central America Report* (Guatemala City), March 2, 1990.
7. For many others, and a comparison sample of reports from Latin America and elsewhere, see *Deterring Democracy,* chap. 10. See also letter 17.
8. *NR,* March 19; *Washington Post,* March 1, 1990.
9. *NYT,* March 2, 1990. On Havel's interesting performance and the enraptured response, see *Deterring Democracy,* 319-20.
10. *NYT* Op-Ed, March 17, 1990.
11. *BG,* Feb. 27, 1990.
12. Maynes, *Foreign Policy,* Spring 1990.

5
Third World, First Threat

April 15, 1990

Dear *LOOT*,

A principle familiar to propagandists is that the doctrines to be instilled in the target audience should not be articulated: that would only expose them to reflection, inquiry, and, very likely, ridicule. The proper procedure is to drill them home by constantly presupposing them, so that they become the very condition for discourse. The technique is illustrated nicely in Michael Gordon's front-page *News of the Week in Review* story in the *New York Times* headlined "Greater Threats from Lesser Powers: the Middle East's Awful Arms Race."[1]

The opening sentence sets the framework: "With the Soviet military threat receding, the spread of chemical, biological and nuclear weapons to the third world is fast emerging as the greatest danger to stability in the world." The statement presupposes what we are to understand as a truism: in the past the Soviet military threat has been the greatest danger to "stability" (a good thing). Now, we are informed, advanced weaponry in the Third World is replacing it.

Crucially, US power never endangered "stability": for example, the resort to direct aggression, subversion, economic warfare and international terrorism in Indochina, Guatemala, the Dominican Republic, Cuba, Nicaragua...; we may stop here, to save some trees. Chile under Allende was an enemy, and therefore not "stable," by definition. Accordingly, there is no self-contradiction when *Foreign Affairs* editor James Chace explains in the *New York Times Magazine* that "our efforts to destabilize a freely elected Marxist government in Chile" illustrate the Nixon-Kissinger efforts "to seek stability."[2]

The basic doctrine is that the state can do no wrong (apart from tactical misjudgment, an excess of benevolence, personal failings, and the like); it is the enemies of the state who are fundamentally evil. A corollary is that US clients are at least on the side of the angels, though sometimes flawed, not quite reaching our unique perfection.

The corollary is illustrated as Gordon proceeds to review the dangers to "stability" in the Third World. In order of importance, these are: missile launchers in Iraq that place Israel under threat; a Libyan capacity to refuel its bombers in flight; an Iraqi threat to wipe out half of Israel if Israel launches a "preemptive strike" (i.e., in response to Israeli aggression); an Iraqi program to develop nuclear weapons within 5 to 10 years (according to Leonard Spector of the Carnegie Endowment); Iranian chemical weapons; Syrian chemical weapons and nerve gas; Libyan chemical weapons; Saudi Arabian medium range missiles; an Egyptian missile project.

In paragraph 17 we reach the final example: "Israel is believed to have a small but potent arsenal of nuclear weapons," as well as missiles that will reach all the Arab states.

So it is the Muslim world that is responsible for "The Middle East's Awful Arms Race." The proliferation threat is becoming "awful" *now*, not thirty years ago when France helped Israel build its Dimona nuclear reactor and, in violation of its pledge, Israel began to use heavy water provided by Norway, then the United States, to produce nuclear weapons there. Similarly, the threat to peace is *Iraq's* effort to obtain high-speed switches to trigger nuclear bombs, not the smuggling of the same devices to Israel years earlier by Los Angeles businessman Richard Smyth, who was indicted on this charge in May 1985, and vanished. Also unthreatening, hence unmentioned here, are the CIA disclosure in 1968 that Israel was producing nuclear weapons and the current estimates that Israel has 100-200 advanced fission bombs and may be adding 10 a year as well as producing the ingredients for thermonuclear weapons. Meanwhile, Israel refuses international inspection and Washington (like Norway) does not exercise its right to inspect and retrieve the heavy water, and with it, the nuclear weapons illegally produced.

Gordon mentions the problem posed by greedy business concerns in Western Europe that sell poison gas ingredients and missile technology to the Arab states and Iran, but missed the efforts by US manufacturers to sell Israel supercomputers that can be used for developing nuclear weapons and long-range delivery systems, along with such matters as the Israeli-South African cooperation on nuclear weapons production and testing for many years.

No less interesting is the failure to mention, here or ever, the reasons why Israel produced nuclear weapons from 1959 with the aid of France, and indirectly, the US and Norway. The responsible French official was Francis Perrin, high commissioner of the French atomic energy agency from 1951 through 1970. He informed the *London Sunday Times* that: "We thought the Israeli bomb was aimed at the Americans, not to launch it against America but to say 'if you don't want to help us in a critical situation we will require you to help us, otherwise we will use our nuclear bombs'." This strategic conception, which can be traced to the mid-1950s, might be of interest to the citizens of the United States, which provides Israel with its high tech (including nuclear) military capacity while blocking a diplomatic settlement of the Arab-Israel conflict. Such matters are taboo, though an assiduous reader can piece bits of the story together from occasional reports.[3]

Also undiscussed is the possible connection between these developments of the past 30 years and the "Greater Threat From Lesser Powers" that is now so ominous. Thus Iraq's possible future threat to Israel arouses great concern, but not Israel's longstanding nuclear threat against the entire Arab world, while it joins with the US in barring a political settlement.

The *Times* has been particularly solicitous in protecting the leading US client state from scrutiny on these (and other) matters. Thus, while Gordon quotes Leonard Spector on the danger that Iraq might obtain nuclear weapons, his warnings over the past years have been treated rather differently.

In 1984, Spector's Carnegie Foundation study of nuclear proliferation identified Israel as "by far the most advanced of eight 'emerging' nuclear powers, surpassing the nuclear capabilities of earlier contenders such as India and South Africa," the *Los Angeles Times* and *Boston Globe* reported. The *Globe* headline read: "Israel may have 20 nuclear arms, Report Says." The *New York Times* story by Richard Halloran the same day is headlined "Nuclear Arms Races in Third World Feared." It mentions Israel once, namely, in having helped to *reduce* the danger of nuclear proliferation by bombing the Iraqi nuclear reactor in 1981. Spector's 1987 study on nuclear proliferation was reported in the *Boston Globe* on page 67, in the Amusements section, under the headline "Report says Israel could 'level' cities," quoting him as saying that Israel may have acquired enough nuclear weaponry "to level every urban center in the Middle East with a population of more than 100,000." The *New York Times* report by Michael Gordon the same day makes no mention of Israel. It opens by warning of *Libyan efforts to acquire* a nuclear capacity, then turns to suspicions about Pakistan, Iran, and India.[4]

When the *London Sunday Times* released Mordechai Vanunu's testimony on Israel's nuclear arsenal in 1986, the *New York Times* looked the other way, eliminating a brief wire service report from its national edition and publishing a few words the next day on Israel's denial of the charges, downplaying the story. Other journals were hardly different, in sharp contrast with European and specialist circles with genuine concern over proliferation. Vanunu's abduction by Israeli intelligence and his secret trial also received little notice, as have the appalling conditions under which he has been held.

Times editors and correspondents are surely not unaware of what they are keeping under wraps. Thus a *Times* Op-Ed by Spector noted that the media have been "surprisingly uncurious" about the Israeli nuclear threat, even after ample evidence had appeared on Israel's nuclear forces and its testing of a nuclear-capable missile with range sufficient to "reach the Soviet Union." He noted further that not a single question was raised to Prime Minister Shamir about this matter in a recent press conference in Washington and TV interviews. The practice largely continues, however, most notably in the Newspaper of Record.[5]

The second major threat that Gordon cites, right after Iraq's potential threat to Israel in years ahead, is Libya's capability to refuel bombers in flight. Not a threat, in contrast, is the US capability to do the same, employed in the terrorist attack against Libya in 1986 on fraudulent pretexts, with dozens of civilians murdered and a most impressive media cover-up that continues until today. Also not a threat is Israel's in-flight refueling capability, which it had used to bomb Tunis six months earlier, killing 75 people with smart bombs that tore them to shreds beyond recognition, among other atrocities described by Israeli journalist Amnon Kapeliouk from the scene, but unreported here. Washington cooperated by failing to warn its ally Tunisia that the bombers were on their way, while, the press reported, George Shultz informed Israeli Foreign Minister Yitzhak Shamir that the US government "had considerable sympathy for the Israeli action," only drawing back from this open approval when the UN Security Council denounced the bombing as an "act of armed aggression" (the US alone abstaining). A few days later Prime Minister Shimon Peres was welcomed to Washington as a man of peace, and the media solemnly reported his discussions with his fellow-pacifist Ronald Reagan on "the evil scourge of terrorism."

The US-Israeli refueling capacity contributes to "stability," and thus constitutes no threat to peace.

Perhaps the most interesting omission is the most obvious one. Is it really a sheer coincidence that Third World
proliferation should suddenly emerge as a major threat to
our existence just at the moment when it is no longer possible to appeal to the Soviet threat as a pretext for intervention abroad and maintaining the public subsidy to high
technology industry through the military system at home?
A journalist interested in pursuing this intriguing question
might turn, for example, to the annual Administration PR
presentations to Congress explaining why we need an even
more elaborate military system than before, with extension
of its industrial base. Particularly interesting was the first
one after the fall of the Berlin Wall in November 1989 eliminated any hope for the ritual appeal to the Soviet threat. The
next Bush Administration National Security Strategy Report, presented to Congress on March 20, 1990, identified
the Third World as the primary locus for potential combat
and as the major threat to US interests, replacing the Soviet
threat; indeed, Soviet power having vanished, we now
learn that the "threats to our interests" in the crucial Middle
East region "could not be laid at the Kremlin's door," contrary to earlier conventions (which are, to be sure, still observed in the loyal media, in what passes for "history" and
"background"). In particular, the Report stated, "The growing technological sophistication of Third World conflicts
will place serious demands on our forces."[6]

In short, we reluctantly concede that the Russians
have departed, taking with them the familiar device to
frighten and mobilize the US public. But we still need huge
military forces, targeting the Third World, which has always been the real enemy, as the actual events of the Cold
War reveal clearly enough. Furthermore, because of the
heights of technological sophistication being achieved by
Third World powers (not without our aid), we still need a
high tech military, including Stealth aircraft to bomb unde-
fended open fields in Panama, SDI to protect us from Iraqi
nukes, etc. Thankfully, there will still be lots of business for

the electronics industry. The other major threat of the day, drugs, also happens to provide a pretext for intervention abroad and repression of the internal Third World at home—fortuitously, no doubt. Some hypotheses can be conjured up without taxing the mind too greatly, but they are not—and are not likely to be—pursued with great vigor.

Sincerely,

Noam

LOOT, 1.5, May 1990

Notes

1. Gordon, *NYT*, April 8. For sources and general background on what follows, see letter 1, note 4. Stephen Green, *Taking Sides* (Morrow, 1984). Mark Gaffney, *Dimona: the Third Temple?* (Amana, 1989). Gary Milhollin, "Heavy Water Cheaters," *Foreign Policy*, Winter 1988-9; *Washington Post Weekly*, April 9-15, 1990. Now also Andrew and Leslie Cockburn, *Dangerous Liaison* (HarperCollins, 1991); Seymour Hersh, *The Samson Option* (Random House, 1991).
2. Chace, "How 'Moral' Can We Get?," *NYT magazine*, May 22, 1977.
3. *London Sunday Times*. Oct. 12, 1986. On Israel's "Samson complex" from the mid-1950s, see *Fateful Triangle*, chap. 7, 4.2.2.
4. *LAT-BG*, *NYT*, Oct. 31, 1984. *BG*, *NYT*, Feb. 25, 1987.
5. Spector, *NYT*, March 17, 1988.
6. AP, March 21, 1990. For further details, see my *Deterring Democracy*, 29f.

6

"Yearning for Democracy"

June 18, 1990

Dear *LOOT*,

The founder of modern Costa Rican democracy, José Figueres, died on June 8 at age 83. His death provided a perfect opportunity for reflection on major themes and events of the past decade and their significance. But to do so honestly would have meant a radical break with cultural and ideological convention. The actual reaction fits the regular practice: to skirt uncomfortable issues that might provide too much understanding of social reality; and to treat people as means, not ends, inverting the moral principles that are granted ritual obeisance while consigned to the ashcan in practice.

For the past decade, a dominant theme of the doctrinal system has been that the traditional benevolence and humanity of US foreign policy is now enhanced by an even-more-passionate-than-usual commitment to democracy, which awakened magically on June 19, 1979 as the Sandinistas overthrew the long-time US favorite Somoza. Indeed, "the yearning to see American-style democracy duplicated throughout the world has been a persistent theme in American foreign policy," *New York Times* diplomatic correspondent Neil Lewis instructed his audience.[1]

Since Central America was the main beneficiary of this yearning, one might expect that the leading figure of Central American democracy, who was quite outspoken about what has been happening, would have achieved a certain prominence during these years. This expectation would only be heightened by a look at his record of support for US state and corporate interests, the usual entry ticket to easy media access. But though superficially plausible, this reasoning fails to recognize the guiding criterion: serviceability to power and privilege. Figueres was simply saying the wrong things, straying beyond the narrow hawk-dove consensus. Accordingly, while occasional mention of "the father of Costa Rican democracy" was permissible in the course of an anti-Sandinista diatribe,[2] those were the limits. For his malfeasance, Figueres had to be virtually censored out of the Free Press.

The *New York Times* carried a lengthy obituary of Figueres by veteran correspondent Eric Pace. The headline reads: "Led Costa Ricans to Democracy." The subheading describes him as "A reformer with a distaste for dictators," referring to his opposition to Trujillo, Somoza, and others like them in the 1950s. An effusive editorial lauded this "fighter for democracy," so forthright that "nobody was in doubt about" his views, such as his bitter opposition to Somoza. More timely and newsworthy indications of his tastes and distastes were somehow missed. It is not hard to figure out why.[3]

In interviews in 1986, Figueres described himself as "pro-Sandinista" and "quite friendly toward the Sandinistas," not because he approved of their particular policies (which were, he said, not his preference), but because "for the first time, Nicaragua has a government that cares for its people." An observer of the 1984 elections, Figueres joined the consensus that was near-universal outside the Washington-media alliance, regarding the elections as free and representative of popular opinion. Returning to Nicaragua two years later, he found "a surprising amount of support for the government" in this "invaded country," adding that the United States should allow the Sandinistas "to finish what they started in peace; they deserve it." He also breached decorum by observing that he "understands why" *La Prensa* was suspended after the virtual US declaration of war against Nicaragua in 1986, having censored the press himself under far less threatening circumstances, when Costa Rica was under attack by Somoza. He did not add the fact—perhaps too obvious to require mention—that the US, Israel, Britain, or other Western democracies would not for a moment tolerate a journal such as *La Prensa*, funded by the terrorist state that had just been condemned by the World Court for its war against Nicaragua and openly supporting that attack.[4]

Compounding his crimes, Figueres not only condemned "Washington's incredible policies of persecuting the Sandinistas" but went on to denounce its efforts "to undo Costa Rica's social institutions" and to "turn our whole economy over to the businesspeople, ... to the local oligarchy or to U.S. or European companies." The United States is "turning most Central Americans into mercenaries" for its attack against Nicaragua, he observed. He was also critical of the Costa Rican media, a virtual monopoly of the ultra-right (hence quite satisfactory to fervent US libertarians).

Useless as a means, the man who "Led Costa Ricans to Democracy" was converted to a nonperson as Central America became an obsession in the 1980s—now returning to its traditional oblivion as elite US interests are considered secure.

It might be thought that at least in an obituary, the truth could be revealed. The Associated Press did permit a phrase noting that Figueres "railed against U.S. policy when the United States supported Nicaragua's Contra guerrillas." But even that gesture was too much for the Newspaper of Record.

Figueres's death offered broader opportunities for the media to provide some understanding of US policies and what lies behind them. It is a commonplace that Costa Rica is an exception to the pattern of terror states that the US has imposed and maintained, with a democratic system on the Western European model. The US reaction has been ambivalent throughout. The record is instructive.

Figueres had his good points. Thus, he was so loyal to US corporations that he was described by the State Department as "the best advertising agency that the United Fruit Company could find in Latin America." He was particularly impressed by the AFL-CIO bureaucrats who have compiled such a successful record in undermining the labor movement abroad while presiding over its decline at home. And he was generally a committed partisan of US actions in Central America, working with the CIA, even lending qualified support to the US invasion of the Dominican Republic in 1965 to bar the constitutionally elected President, Juan Bosch. He supported the Bay of Pigs invasion, anticipating "a quick victory by the democratic forces which have gone into Cuba," and later expressed his regrets for their "lamentable" defeat. He was concerned only that his enemy Trujillo be deposed first, after which the Dominican Republic could be used as a base against Castro. Pace quotes him as expressing opposition to the invasion, but omits the relevant background.

More crucially, Figueres adhered faithfully to the US conception of "democracy" as unchallenged rule by business with the general population marginalized. He recognized early on that the Costa Rican Communist Party, particularly strong among plantation workers, was posing an unacceptable challenge. He therefore arrested its leaders, declared the party illegal, and repressed its members, a policy that was maintained through the 1960s, as efforts to establish any working class party were banned by the state authorities. He also explained the reasons with candor: It was "a sign of weakness. I admit it, when one is relatively weak before the force of the enemy, it is necessary to have the valor to recognise it." These moves were accepted in the West as consistent with the liberal concept of democracy, and indeed, were virtually a precondition for US toleration of "the Costa Rican exception."

In general, Figueres aligned himself unequivocally with the United States. His government provided a favorable climate for foreign investment, suppressed labor and political dissidence, and guaranteed the domestic predominance of business interests.

Nevertheless, the US remained dissatisfied. Though the Constitution outlawed the Communist Party and labor was effectively repressed, Costa Rica still fell short of US standards of democracy and freedom. Eisenhower's Ambassador Robert Woodward warned that "the commies" had not been completely rooted out of "the laboring class," and there had been "no move to stamp out the movement completely." Furthermore, Costa Rica remained committed to free expression and to legal rights that made it difficult to arrest Communists and suppress their publications, as a solid commitment to democracy would require. The State Department was critical of Costa Rica's respect for civil liberties, the "lackadaisical...attitude of the government toward [the] suppression" of communists, and the failure of the media to rely sufficiently on US sources. The Kennedy Administration was troubled more generally by the excessive liberalism of Latin American countries and their failure to trim democratic forms to the overriding needs of domestic and foreign business interests.

During the 1980s, with the lash of the debt to ensure obedience, and with the cooperation of pro-business leaders such as Oscar Arias, the US dedicated itself to unravelling the social welfare programs, rebuilding the army (under a different name), and in general restoring Costa Rica to the favored "Central American mode." In Figueres's unreportable words, the US is attempting "to undo Costa Rica's social institutions, to turn our whole economy over to the businesspeople, and to do away with our social insurance, our nationalized bank, our nationalized electric utility—the few companies we have that are too large to be in private hands. The United States is trying to force us to sell them to so-called private enterprise, which means turning them over to the local oligarchy or to U.S. or European companies."

The death of Figueres offers other opportunities for timely reflection. The "Costa Rican exception" was based on state-led economic development with social expenditures to benefit much of the population; that is to say, it radically violated the prescriptions that the US and the international institutions it dominates seek to impose on "developing countries," including now Eastern Europe. More generally, reliance on state power and coordination in violation of market principles has been a universal feature of successful economic development, from England to South Korea and Taiwan, including the US itself. The doctrines advocated for—and when possible imposed upon—the Third World are not based on the empirical evidence on economic development, though they do admirably serve the needs of local elites and foreign corporations, facts that might elicit some thought, if that deviation from decorum were permissible.

José Figueres's career, and the US reaction to him, has much to teach about Central America and about the fabled "yearning for democracy" that so inspires US elites. Better, then, to suppress it in favor of a more serviceable story, all the way to the grave.

Sincerely,

Noam

LOOT, 1.7, July 1990

Notes

1. Lewis, *NYT*, Dec. 6, 1987.
2. James LeMoyne, *NYT Magazine*, Jan. 10, 1988.
3. Pace, *NYT*, June 9; editorial, *NYT*, June 17, 1990. For sources on what follows, and background on Figueres and US relations with Costa Rica generally, see *Necessary Illusions*, 111f. and App. V.1. Also Anthony Winson, *Coffee & Modern Costa Rican Democracy* (St. Martin's Press, 1989).
4. See *Necessary Illusions*, App. V.6-7, on the utterly cynical manipulation of the *La Prensa* issue by US media and the "intellectual community" generally, and on their real commitments concerning freedom of press, too revealing and well-confirmed to be allowed to see the light of day.

7

Apostles of Nonviolence

July 18, 1990

Dear *LOOT*,

"There's No Tolerating Terror," the *New York Times* editors admonished the Bush Administration, then wrestling with its painful responsibilities as guardian of international morality after a failed guerrilla operation by a PLO faction. The Bush Administration had already announced that the US would never "countenance terrorism," but it was still hoping to keep the "peace process" alive, despite this proof of PLO iniquity. Columnist Anthony Lewis, regularly denounced for his pro-Palestinian bias, warned Yasser Arafat that "the time for fudging has run out": no terrorist should be permitted "on the executive committee of an organization committed to negotiation and peace with Israel."[1]

Though it is uplifting to watch the *Times* pursue its inspiring crusade to instruct its adversaries in the principles of Gandhi and Martin Luther King—whose names are regularly invoked in lectures to the Mandelas and the Arafats who have not reached our lofty pinnacle in this regard—nevertheless some flickers of uncertainty remain.

In his admonition to Arafat, Lewis states that "Palestinians can make political progress only by convincing Israel of their desire for negotiation and peace." The presupposition is that Israel desires such an outcome, but is deterred by Palestinian intransigence. The facts, as we have seen, are quite different. Egyptian president Sadat's offer of a full peaceful settlement was not considered until after the 1973 war had revealed that the post-1967 triumphalism of Israel and its US patron was built on sand, and was then converted into a device to facilitate Israel's takeover of the occupied territories and aggression against Lebanon. Israel withdrew from most of Lebanon only when violent resistance raised the costs too high. When the population of the territories seemed quiescent under the boot of the military and the settlers, suffering regular terror, torture, and humiliation, there was no thought of compromise there. From the early days of the Zionist movement, Arab moderation has been regarded as more of a threat than Arab militancy. Both political groupings in Israel have always been firmly opposed to meaningful negotiations with Palestinians, and the "peace process" that they and Washington advance is founded on the clear and explicit rejection of Palestinian national rights.

These facts being unacceptable, the media have been careful to keep them under wraps—indeed, to falsify them (as Lewis does, though he is less extreme than most). Remarkably, even the actual terms of the Peres-Shamir-Baker plan have not passed through the media filter, though it is official US policy, regularly described as "the only game in town" and of great significance. These achievements should inspire no small amount of respect.[2]

Let us put all this aside, however, and turn to terrorism, beginning with a conceptual point. What is it? Two different responses are relevant in the present connection: international conventions, and what we may call "the South African exception." The first version is formulated clearly in the UN General Assembly resolution of December 1987 condemning terrorism in all its forms, while stating that "the struggle for self-determination, freedom and independence" against "colonial or racist regimes" or "foreign occupation" does not fall under the rubric of terrorism. The South African exception rejects this clause. On this issue, world opinion is divided. The UN resolution passed 153 to 2, with the US and Israel opposed (Honduras abstaining). The facts again passed without report, it being understood, across the spectrum, that when the world is out of step it is simply irrelevant.

Also unmentioned is that it is precisely this issue that lies behind the solemn deliberations about granting the PLO entry to the "dialogue"—in reality, a monologue in which these miscreants are granted the right to listen to US demands that they quietly fade away. PLO acceptance of the near-universal international consensus on terrorism was angrily denounced as "the old Arafat hedge" by the *Times* editors, with Anthony Lewis, again at the dissident extreme, calling on Arafat to prove his seriousness by affirming the South African exception with greater clarity than he had yet shown. If there were deviations from this pattern in the media chorus, I failed to find them.[3]

Let us adopt the Party Line on this matter too, and proceed—not without noting, however, that we are now entering realms of subservience to state power that go well beyond the disgraceful norm. Recalling that terrorists must be rigorously excluded from the PLO executive to satisfy the stern Washington-media standards, we naturally ask whether the same injunction applies to Israel (we may dismiss those extremists who might harbor a subversive thought about the master of ceremonies). If not, one might ask why. If so, some further questions quickly arise. The terrorist career of Prime Minister Shamir extends back half a century. A leading figure in his cabinet is Ariel Sharon, who does, in fact, figure in *New York Times* deliberations on terrorism—as an expert on how to combat the plague; see Sharon's Op-Ed, "It's Past Time to Crush The Terrorist Monster," advising that only by violence can we "Stop the slaughter of innocents."[4] Sharon does not lack experience in these matters. He has been organizing terrorist atrocities since the early 1950s, the best-known early case (though not the first) being the vicious massacre at Qibya in 1953; or we might mention his "regime of indiscriminate terror" in Gaza in 1971 (Amnon Dankner),[5] an example with obvious relevance to the current version of these practices supervised by the US favorites.

But let us put these hesitations aside as well, removing

from the agenda the mounting wave of sadistic repression and totalitarian rule in the territories, recorded in the Hebrew press and human rights reports, but scarcely visible to those who pay the bills.

Another question is raised by Robert Fisk, the veteran British Middle East correspondent. "More than 100 people were killed in Israeli air raids on Lebanon last year, many of them civilians," he writes. "Palestinians might be forgiven for asking why President Bush does not break off relations with Israel when it bombs a Palestinian camp in Lebanon. But the PLO knows this would have been outside the bounds of political reality."[6] Equally outside the bounds is possibility that the cultural managers might permit the thought to be expressed here.

The air raids to which Fisk refers are well north of Israel's "security zone" in Lebanon, where the harsh repression by Israel's terrorist mercenary army (the SLA) backed by Israeli force is also off the American agenda. We therefore need not tarry on the bombardment of market places, schools, and hospitals, the torture and sieges to deprive recalcitrant villagers of sustenance, the early morning raids by Israeli troops to expel women and children from villages that refuse to submit to the rule of the chosen collaborators, and other atrocities condemned by the Norwegian UN forces, who vainly try to protect the inhabitants, as "inhuman acts" that are reminiscent of methods used by the Nazis, to mention a few cases from the period when every word of Arafat's was being closely scrutinized to see if he had truly joined us off the spectrum of world opinion by adopting the South African exception and could thus be admitted to a "dialogue."[7] The story continues, with no question raised about admissibility of the US client state to negotiations or its qualifications for a huge subsidy.

No contradiction is stark enough to disturb the equanimity of the arbiters of good behavior. Thus Robert Pear reports a US warning to the PLO that the "dialogue" will be endangered unless the PLO adheres rigorously to the South

African exception. "Attacks against Israeli civilian or military targets inside or outside of Israel are contrary to the peaceful objectives of the dialogue," State Department spokesman Charles Redman announced, referring to an incident in which three Palestinian guerrillas were killed in an attack on Israeli soldiers and SLA mercenaries in southern Lebanon. "The P.L.O. cannot escape responsibility" in such cases, Redman warned. A brief story on the adjacent page reports that Israeli jets bombed Palestinian targets near Beirut, far north of the region occupied by Israel and its mercenary army, killing three people and wounding 22 schoolchildren when a missile hit a schoolyard. "Panicked children aged four to 10, some with blood streaming down their faces, ran screaming and sobbing from the school," AP reported, adding that five were critically injured. No warnings were issued to Israel, though there was a US reaction. Charles Redman stated that "this latest sequence of actions and reaction in south Lebanon [sic] underscores once again the need for agreed on security arrangements."[8]

Times editors and columnists issued no stern admonitions, and saw no incongruities.

So matters continue. To take a few cases, several weeks later, in late March, Israeli planes killed 20 people in a farming community east of Beirut, including an entire Lebanese family buried under the rubble and other civilians (*NYT, WP*). In October, the SLA expelled 28 Lebanese from Israel's "security zone" because three of their relatives had defected from the mercenary force (AP). In December, SLA gunners shelled the market town of Nabatiyeh, killing three civilians and wounding nine (AP). In February 1990, Israeli warplanes attacked Palestinian targets near Sidon, with a second attack as casualties were evacuated, the usual tactic (AP). The purpose was to deter actions against Israeli troops in southern Lebanon, the army announced. Further raids in July received some attention, perhaps because they "raised fears that reported plans for the release of a Western hostage held here could be delayed," Hijazi reported. Other actions, such as Israel's regular practice of hijacking civilian vessels in international waters, passed with little notice, as always.[9]

In an article on American hostages in Lebanon, Thomas Friedman reported that some were abducted "in order to get a third party, Israel, to free more than 300 Lebanese Shiites being held in prisons in south Lebanon" and other political prisoners, including "Sheikh Abdel Karim Obeid, who was kidnapped by Israel in July [1989]." A Shiite Muslim leader who had played a role in the release of Robert Polhill added that freeing these prisoners was "essential" for any further progress on the hostages (AP). Meanwhile the British press reported on the worst of these prisons, the horror chamber at Khiam (Ansar I) established during the invasion of Lebanon and used since to punish people suspected of anti-Israel activity in Lebanon, or their relatives, some held for five years according to UN records, after having been brought there by Israeli secret police (Shin Beth) agents. Local inhabitants believe that the purpose is "to inspire terror in the local Lebanese population"—with considerable success, Robert Fisk reports. Neither the International Red Cross nor any other humanitarian organization has been allowed to visit Khiam, but there is ample evidence of hideous conditions and savage torture of inmates by Israel's proxies under Israeli supervision, according to numerous independent and consistent testimonies. Julie Flint, reporting a separate inquiry, adds that "the prison is at last getting international attention [outside the United States, that is] because Iran has linked the release of Khiam's inmates to the continued freeing of Western hostages," a story that matters.[10]

It would be misleading simply to accuse the US government and media of a double standard in ignoring Israel's terrorist operations while bitterly condemning any action against Israeli military targets, even in Lebanon. Rather, we must understand that the South African exception is complemented by a deeper principle. Terrorist acts by the

United States and its clients are automatically excluded from the canon. Once the terminology is understood, we see that a single standard prevails; there is no inconsistency.

On the same grounds, we can understand why the chief diplomatic correspondent of the *New York Times* should approve of Israel's savagery in Lebanon. Shortly after receiving his second Pulitzer Prize for Middle East reporting, Thomas Friedman, in interviews in Israel, proposed the brutal Israeli-run regime of south Lebanon as a model for the occupied territories. But Friedman is a noted dove, and accordingly added a qualification: The Palestinians should be granted some crumbs, he urged, because "only if you give the Palestinians something to lose is there a hope that they will agree to moderate their demands," abandoning the ludicrous hope for mutual recognition in a two-state settlement—a "demand" that Friedman refused to report and consistently denied while producing the "balanced and informed coverage" for which he received the prize. "I believe that as soon as Ahmed has a seat in the bus, he will limit his demands," Friedman added.[11]

One might ask what the reaction would be if a prominent journalist urged South Africans to "give Sambo a seat in the bus," or proposed that Jews be granted something to lose, because "if you give Hymie a seat in the bus, he may limit his demands." Promotion to chief diplomatic correspondent, perhaps?

Sincerely,

Noam

LOOT, 1.8, August 1990

Notes

1. Editorial, *NYT*, June 13; Thomas Friedman, *NYT*, June 9; Anthony Lewis, *NYT*, "Arafat to Choose," June 5, 1990.
2. On Sadat and Camp David, see letter 1; on the Peres-Shamir-Baker plan, letter 12. For general background, see references of letter 1, note 4. On Middle East terrorism, and terrorism in

the real world generally, see *Necessary Illusions* (*NI*), *Pirates & Emperors*. Also Edward S. Herman and Gerry O'Sullivan, *The 'Terrorism' Industry* (Pantheon, 1990), and earlier works of Herman's cited there; and Alexander George, ed., *Western State Terrorism* (Polity, 1991).

3. Editorial, *NYT*, Nov. 16, 1988; Lewis, "Include Us Out," *NYT*, Dec. 1, 1988. See *NI*, App. V.4, for details.

4. Sharon, *NYT*, Sept. 30, 1986.

5. *Hadashot*, April 11, 1989.

6. *Independent*, June 25, 1990.

7. For details, see *NI*, 192f.

8. Pear, "Halt Raids on Israel or Put Ties at Risk, U.S. Tells the PLO," *NYT*, A7; Ihsan Hijazi, "Israeli Bomb Hits Lebanon School," *NYT*, A6, March 1, 1990. AP, *Boston Globe*, Feb. 28, 1989. Redman, Reuters, *BG*, March 1, 1989.

9. Ihsan Hijazi, *NYT*, March 21; Nora Boustany, *Washington Post*, March 21; AP, Oct. 25, December 2, 1989. AP, Feb. 19, 1990. Ihsan Hijazi, *NYT*, July 9, 10, 1990.

10. Friedman, "For the Captors, Less In Common with Iran," *NYT*, April 24; AP, April 25; Robert Fisk, *Independent*, April 20; Julie Flint, *Observer*, May 13, 1990. On the early days of Israel's torture chamber at Khiam, see *Fateful Triangle, Pirates & Emperors*.

11. *Yediot Ahronot*, April 7, 1988; *Hotam*, April 15, 1988. See *NI*, 294f.

8
UN = US

September 6, 1990

Dear *LOOT*,

It's no easy matter to find anything to relieve the gloom of the Gulf crisis, but the media have found one ray of light: the sudden improvement in the behavior of the United Nations. The *Boston Globe* hailed "The U.N.'s coming of age" with a new mood of responsibility and seriousness. A news report explained further that "Moscow's quick condemnation of the [Iraqi] invasion freed the U.N. Security Council, long paralyzed by superpower rivalry, to play a critical role" in responding to the aggression (Pamela Constable). Given these new circumstances, *Times* correspondent R.W. Apple added, Washington is "leaning harder in its policy-making on the United Nations, now more functional than in decades because of the passing of the cold war."[1]

The background was reviewed by John Goshko in the *Washington Post*. The UN has been "transformed" into an agency for world peace "after years of being dismissed as a failure and a forum for Third World demagoguery" during "the long Cold War rivalry between the United States and the Soviet Union and their allies." Hopes for the UN were "thwarted from the outset by the bitter Cold War between the United States and the Soviet Union. In those early years, the images of the United Nations that became engraved on the world's consciousness were of grim-faced Soviet ambassadors casting vetoes or storming out of Security Council meetings." Later, the new Third World members "turned the [General] Assembly into a forum for frequently shrill, anti-Western rhetoric." But "about two years ago, a change began to set in as the result of the détente-oriented changes in Soviet foreign policy." Now we have reached a "rare

moment for the United Nations," which "is suddenly working the way it was designed to."[2]

Post political commentator David Broder added his
imprimatur: "During the long Cold War years, the Soviet
veto and the hostility of many Third World nations made
the United Nations an object of scorn to many American
politicians and citizens. But in today's altered environment,
it has proved to be an effective instrument of world leadership, and, potentially, an agency that can effect both peace
and the rule of law in troubled regions."[3]

In brief, the UN misbehaved in the past because of
superpower rivalry, Russian obstructionism, and the psychic disorders of the Third World. But our victory in the
Cold War has changed all that.

One hates to be a killjoy, but there does seem to be
something missing. It's true enough that 40 years ago
"grim-faced Soviet ambassadors" were vetoing resolutions,
for reasons that might be worth at least brief mention. To
skip from then to 1988 is, perhaps, also a bit facile; and a few
words might be in order about the past several decades as
well. Let's add some of the missing pieces, and see what
happens to this pleasant tale.

There still are Security Council vetoes, and votes in
isolation against General Assembly resolutions. To mention
a few cases having to do with the Middle East, in June 1990,
the US vetoed a resolution (voted 14-1) calling for a fact-
finding mission to investigate abuses against Palestinians in
the occupied territories. Going back "about two years," as
we are advised, in early 1988 the US vetoed a series of
resolutions condemning Israeli attacks on Lebanon, propos-
ing a UN role in peace negotiations, and calling on Israel to
abide by the Geneva conventions. In October, the General
Assembly condemned Israel for "killing and wounding defenseless Palestinians" by a vote of 130 to 2 (US, Israel). In
June 1989, the US again vetoed a resolution deploring
Israel's violation of Palestinian human rights. According to
one estimate, the US has vetoed 23 of 66 Security Council

resolutions on these issues.[4]

To mention a few other cases of obvious relevance, the United States was alone (with Israel) in opposing a General Assembly resolution calling for an end to hostilities when Israel invaded Lebanon in June 1982. The US vetoed Security Council resolutions condemning Israel for ignoring the UN's demand for the withdrawal of its forces, and calling for simultaneous withdrawal of Israeli and Palestinian armed forces from Beirut, then just coming under devastating Israeli bombardment of civilian targets; the latter veto was justified on the grounds that the resolution "was a transparent attempt to preserve the P.L.O. as a viable political force," plainly unacceptable, since a major goal of this US-backed aggression was to undermine the embarrassing diplomatic initiatives of the PLO, as explained clearly in Israel from the outset, but barred from the record here.

Two months earlier, the US had vetoed a resolution calling on Israel to reinstate three elected mayors who had been recent targets of Jewish terrorist attacks (April 2, 13-1, Zaire abstaining). On the same day, the US vetoed a resolution calling upon the Secretary-General to keep the Council informed about the crisis in Central America, with no names or charges, but implicitly directed against US intervention in Nicaragua. The resolution "breeds cynicism" and "harms the United Nations" because it "undermines the Inter-American system" and "mocks the search for peace," the US delegation protested; Saddam Hussein adopted exactly the same stance in condemning UN resolutions about Kuwait which (he claimed) undermine the Arab peace-keeping system, eliciting much righteous indignation. Observers in April 1982 could recall no previous occasion when one country cast two vetoes on two different subjects on a single day.

Only a few months before Iraq's invasion of Kuwait, the US, in routine fashion, vetoed a resolution condemning Israel's practices in the occupied territories (November 1989, voted 14-1). Shortly after, the US voted (alone with

Israel) against a General Assembly resolution condemning
its support for the contra army attacking Nicaragua; and,
again alone with Israel, voted against a resolution opposing
the illegal embargo against Nicaragua (December 1989). In
January, the US (alone) vetoed a Security Council resolution
condemning its attack on the Nicaraguan Embassy in Panama (13-1, Britain abstaining).

By an odd oversight, the *Times* editors forgot the last
of these examples in an outraged editorial after Saddam
Hussein had surrounded foreign embassies in Kuwait with
troops. The editors denounced this scoundrel, now de-
scending to truly unspeakable acts, for "lash[ing] out at
diplomacy itself." They demanded, for the first time, that he
be tried as a war criminal under the Nuremberg principles.
The charges included his defiance of international law and
treaties, "ill treatment of civilians in occupied territories,"
and now this new outrage against "diplomats whose special status is protected by the Vienna Conventions."[5] The
charges are valid, and perhaps those guilty of them should
indeed be tried under Nuremberg principles as the *Times*
editors demand, including the invader of Panama and man-
ager of what the World Court called "the unlawful use of
force" against Nicaragua, and the US ally that the editors
describe as the very "symbol of human decency," "a society
in which moral sensitivity is a principle of political life"—
standard media fare with regard to Israel (as long as it is
following orders, that is). Strangely, the editors overlooked
these corollaries to the principles they so stoutly defend.

Details of the kind just briefly sampled (I stress, *sampled)* are generally unreported or dismissed with a wave of
the hand, but not always. Thus, the impassioned words of
US Ambassador Thomas Pickering in support of the Security Council resolution condemning Iraq rekindled some
recent memories for one Washington correspondent, who
recalled the Security Council resolution of December 23,
1989 condemning the US invasion of Panama (vetoed by the
US, with British and French assistance, in this case), and the

General Assembly resolution of December 29, 1990 demanding the withdrawal of the "US armed invasion forces from Panama" and calling the invasion a "flagrant violation of international law and of the independence, sovereignty and territorial integrity of states." Fortunately, his words appeared only in Dublin, not disturbing the required unanimity where it mattered.[6] Closer to home, the insight seems to have been missed—along with the facts.

Turning to some other relevant areas, while Ronald Reagan was being extolled (in the US) for leading the world towards peace at the December 1987 Washington summit, where the INF treaty was signed, the General Assembly voted a series of disarmament resolutions. It voted 154 to 1, with no abstentions, opposing weapons in outer space (Reagan's Star Wars), 135 to 1 against developing new weapons of mass destruction, 143 to 2 for a comprehensive test ban, and 137 to 3 for a halt to all nuclear test explosions. As usual, there was one "grim-faced ambassador" who voted against each resolution, joined in two cases by France, and one by Britain. None of this was reported in the national press—though General Assembly votes critical of the Soviet Union were prominently reported at exactly that time. The disarmament votes were obviously timely, given the outpouring of praise for Reagan the Peacemaker, but hardly useful. The *New York Times*, *Washington Post*, and the three TV networks also managed to overlook a General Assembly resolution at the same session calling for "full and immediate compliance" with the World Court condemnation of the US war against Nicaragua (the US and Israel opposed). A similar resolution a year earlier (US, Israel, and El Salvador opposed) had also passed unnoticed, though there was a brief report in the *Times* when the US vetoed a Security Council resolution calling on all states to observe international law.

The US has repeatedly vetoed Security Council resolutions, voted against General Assembly resolutions (often alone, or virtually so), and blocked UN initiatives on a whole range of issues, including disarmament and peace, international law, terrorism, the Middle East, South Africa, protection of the environment, and others. The US is far in the lead since 1970 in vetoing Security Council resolutions (Britain second, France a distant third), and in rejecting General Assembly resolutions in (virtual) isolation. The grim-faced ambassadors casting vetoes have had good American accents, while the USSR has regularly voted with the overwhelming majority. US isolation would, in fact, have been more severe, were it not for its unmatched power, which kept major issues from the UN agenda. The Soviet invasion of Afghanistan was bitterly censured, but the UN was never willing to take on the US war against Indochina.

Though the facts and their significance are not considered fit for discussion, or even report for the most part, the aberrant behavior of the world does occasionally elicit some puzzled commentary. *Times* UN correspondent Richard Bernstein pondered the deterioration of international norms from the good old days when there was "an automatic majority" supporting US positions. He attributes this moral decline to "the very structure and political culture" of the UN and the lack of diplomatic skills among the bluff Americans, whose simple-minded honesty, we are to understand, does not equip them for the machinations of devious forces beyond our borders.[7] In the early years, before the decay set it, an "automatic majority" was guaranteed by the enormous preponderance of US wealth and power in a world that had been devastated by the war. The UN could therefore be used as a weapon against the Soviet enemy, and regularly was, leading to Soviet vetoes. This deviant Soviet behavior was subjected to close scrutiny by Western scholars, from anthropologists to political analysts, who sought to find some explanation for it. There were sober inquiries into the strange negativism of the Russians, attributed by some thinkers to their practice of swaddling infants—what the handful of skeptics used to call "diaperology." Later, as the organization fell under "the tyranny of the majority" (a.k.a. "democracy"), the "shrill, anti-Western rhetoric" of demented Third Worlders came under similar investigation, along with the curious refusal of the industrial world to "join the team"—"the team" being Washington, even if it is entirely alone—perhaps a reflection of their uncertainties and resentments over our magnificence, as Bernstein and others suggested.

The UN is a good little boy when it is following our orders. That was true in the early postwar years, given the conditions of the time, and again in the current Gulf crisis (more or less; in fact, much less than is pretended). This has little to do with the Cold War, the Russians, or the Third World.

The conclusion is so salient that it could not possibly be missed. But it would be a mistake to charge the media with deceit for failing to articulate what must be entirely obvious to every commentator. Rather, the apparent facts run counter to a deeper principle of logic, and therefore are not really facts, despite appearances. Certain truths are uncontroversial, as demonstrated conclusively by the fact that they are put forth by US power. If the community of nations fails to comprehend this, we naturally inquire into the cultural or psychic disorders from which they suffer. The media are only behaving responsibly, then, when they ignore the actual history in favor of self-serving fairy tales.

The basic point was explained during the Kennedy years by the highly respected political scientist Hans Morgenthau, the founder of the tough-minded "realist" school, which keeps to hard fact and concrete power relations, scorning sentimentality and illusion. Actual history, Morgenthau wrote, is only "the abuse of reality." "Reality itself" is revealed by "the evidence of history as our minds reflect it," and it is a simple error of logic to confuse the two.[8] Once this is understood, all falls into place.

Sincerely,

Noam

Notes

1. Editorial, *BG*, Aug. 8; Constable, *BG*, Aug. 20. Apple, *NYT*, Aug. 21, 1990.
2. Goshko, *WP Weekly*, Sept. 3, 1990.
3. Broder, *Ibid.*
4. AP, June 1, 1990; not reported in *New York Times*; Cheryl Rubenberg, *Arab Studies Quarterly*, Fall 1989; Nabeel Abraham, *American-Arab Affairs*, Winter 1989-90. For details on cases cited below, see my *Culture of Terrorism* (South End, 1988), 195; *Necessary Illusions*, 82f. 218ff.; *Fateful Triangle*, 9, 114. On UN and Lebanon, see Sally V. Mallison and W. Thomas Mallison, *Armed Conflict in Lebanon* (American Educational Trust, 1985), 94, 104; T. Mallison and S. Mallison, *The Palestine Problem in International Law and World Order* (Longman, 1986), 477-79. On US-UN relations in late 1990-1991, see letter 12. For further detail, my chapter in Cynthia Peters, ed., *Collateral Damage* (South End, 1992), and *Deterring Democracy*. Relevant scholarship is slim, even the basic documents are hard to obtain, and the media and commentators largely ignore the UN unless it can serve as an ideological weapon.
5. Editorial, *NYT*, Aug. 25, 1990.
6. Sean Cronin, *Irish Times*, Aug. 11, 1990.
7. "The U.N. versus the U.S.," *NYT magazine*, Jan. 22, 1984. Note that it is not the U.S. versus the U.N., with a crucially different connotation.
8. Morgenthau, *The Purpose of American Politics* (Vintage, 1964); see *Towards a New Cold War*, 73f.

9
Postscript: "Riding Moynihan's Hobby Horse"

September 6, 1990

Dear *LOOT*,

A postscript to my last letter, in which I reviewed the miraculous transformation of the United Nations from scoundrel to agency for world peace as it (partially) conformed to US wishes instead of engaging in its usual childish pursuits: Calling on the US and its clients to observe international law and to refrain from aggression, annexation, and abuse of civilians; advocating disarmament; and otherwise compelling the US to uphold order by regularly vetoing Security Council resolutions and rejecting General Assembly resolutions, alone or with some client state.

Just when one thinks that hypocrisy has reached the outer limits, something happens to reveal the naiveté of such faith. Accordingly, a few days after I wrote, the *New York Times Magazine* ran a story by James Traub on Daniel Patrick Moynihan, who, we learn, is "taking particular delight" in being proven right in his heroic advocacy of international law and the United Nations system, "abstractions" that "matter dearly" to him, Traub reports with awe.[1] Finally, at last, everybody is "riding Moynihan's hobbyhorse" instead of ignoring the principles he has upheld with such conviction for so many years. No longer need Moynihan "revel in his martyrdom." At last, "history has caught up with him." The just are vindicated, as in fairy tales.

Even before this ode was published, Senator Moynihan had been produced as an expert witness on "the new spirit of unanimity at the United Nations."[2] There were "some pretty egregious violations of international law in the past," Moynihan explained, but now "the major powers have convergent interests and the mechanism of the U.N. is there waiting to be used." Moynihan's forthright advocacy of these mechanisms had also been lauded in reviews of a recent book. But the *Magazine* story reaches new heights of adulation for his courage and integrity in upholding international law and the UN system.

It makes good sense for Moynihan to be approached on these topics. After all, he had direct experience as UN Ambassador, when he had ample opportunity to put his principles into practice. Checking its files, the *Times* could have found a cablegram to Henry Kissinger on January 23, 1976, in which Moynihan reported with pride on the "considerable progress" he had achieved with his arm-twisting tactics "toward a basic foreign policy goal, that of breaking up the massive blocs of nations, mostly new nations, which for so long have been arrayed against us in international forums and in diplomatic encounters generally."[3] Moynihan was particularly proud of two cases that are highly relevant to Iraq's invasion of Kuwait, the issue that he is now called upon to discuss: his success in undermining any UN reaction to the Indonesian invasion of East Timor and to Moroccan aggression in the Sahara, both supported by the US, the former with particular vigor.

If checking its files was too much work, the *Times* could have looked at Moynihan's memoir of his years at the United Nations.[4] Here, he describes frankly his role as Indonesia invaded East Timor in December 1975:

> The United States wished things to turn out as they did, and worked to bring this about. The Department of State desired that the United Nations prove utterly ineffective in whatever measures it undertook. This task was given to me, and I carried it forward with no inconsiderable success.

He adds that within a few weeks some 60,000 people had been killed, "10 percent of the population, almost the proportion of casualties experienced by the Soviet Union during the Second World War." No wonder he took such pride in his achievement.

We need not review here the rest of the story, until today, as the US and its allies have provided military and diplomatic support for atrocities on a scale that make Iraq's invasion of Kuwait look like a tea party in comparison while the media pretended not to see—hardly the only such case. Nor need we tarry over the appeal by Portugal's Prime Minister on September 14, 1990 reminding the world community that Indonesia's invasion and annexation of East Timor is no less outrageous than the exploit that ended Washington's love affair with Saddam Hussein.[5] The foolish Portuguese official is one of those "arrayed against us" in our crusade for world order, and therefore merits no more comment than he received.

One can appreciate the need to sweep under the rug such embarrassments as the US attitude towards the UN system and international law in Panama, Nicaragua, Grenada, Cyprus, Namibia, Lebanon, and on and on. But it takes real talent to select as heroic defender of these principles someone who has been so frank and outspoken in recalling his actions to demolish them.

Meanwhile, the farce proceeds as expected. *Times* UN correspondent Paul Lewis explained that "with the Soviet Union no longer automatically siding with the enemies of the United States, the Security Council already finds itself at the center of world attention as it starts to function as it was supposed to, compelling countries to settle differences peacefully."[6] To translate from *Times*-speak to English: For once, the US is not undermining UN efforts to enforce the principles we preach, isolated (or virtually so) in opposition to the international community while the USSR votes with the large majority, including US allies.

The same day, the *Times* editors gaze in awe at the "wondrous sea change" as the UN finally gets serious, silencing "most of its detractors"; and they hail President Bush for his noble effort to create a "new world order to resolve conflicts by multilateral diplomacy and collective security"—without a word on the dedicated work of George Bush and his predecessors (always with the loyal aid of the *New York Times)* to ensure that nothing of the sort would be possible. When Bush denounced Iraq at the UN for having "plundered Kuwait, terrorized innocent civilians, and held even diplomats hostage," warning of dire consequences, the *Times* editors praised him for his statesmanship, falsely claiming that he had proposed a "diplomatic solution"; he had unequivocally and firmly *rejected* any diplomatic solution, dismissing without consideration Iraqi offers considered "serious" and "negotiable" by the high US officials who leaked them to the *Times*, which obediently suppressed the facts it knew (as it conceded in the small print when exposed).[7]

Needless to say, the editors do not see fit to mention other recent actions fitting George Bush's eloquent denunciation of Iraq, carried out by the US or its clients while the UN stood by helpless in the face of US obstruction. This has been the common pattern for many years. But it is not useful, therefore not part of history.

Despite the "wondrous sea change," diplomatic correspondent Thomas Friedman warns, all is not yet perfect. Many of our partners have joined the grand coalition that Bush has forged "only because of a coincidence of interest, not because they share a common sense of moral purpose." Hence the coalition is "a fragile one," limiting "Washington's room for maneuver" in pursuit of the high moral purpose that animates it, unlike its unworthy allies.[8]

Similarly the *Boston Globe*, while commending Gorbachev for his progress, warns that "as with France, Japan, Israel or Egypt, the contributions of the Soviet ally are circumscribed by unique national interests"—unlike us, alone in our sublimity, the reader is to understand.[9]

The *Globe* editors are optimistic that the Russians may progress further. "The day is not far off," they hope, "when the Kremlin can assume its long-sought role as a peacemaker in the Mideast." Perhaps they will finally see the light and join us, relieving our isolation off the spectrum of world opinion by abandoning their disruptive advocacy of the political settlement of the Arab-Israel conflict that has been sought by virtually the entire world for many years, and blocked only by Washington's unremitting rejectionism. Then they too will be "peacemakers," helping to bar the path to peace.

One might ask what difference it makes if the media do their little pirouettes. It matters a great deal. Suppose that the US were indeed upholding high principle in pursuit of its historic mission, now finally joined by much of the world (though, of course, for shabby motives, not sharing our moral purpose). Then conceivably, a case might be made—however thin—for Washington's course: undermining any diplomatic track, rejecting the appeals of its allies (UK aside) and the Iraqi democratic opposition that it pursue peaceful means as prescribed by international law, and scorning the advice of UN Secretary General Perez de Cuellar that "there is room for negotiations."[10] And, of course, warding off any thought of free elections in Kuwait after Iraqi withdrawal (which would "reward Saddam Hussein for aggression"), or other equally atrocious suggestions. The argument would be: It is wrong to compromise on the lofty principles that one has always staunchly upheld. The suppressed historical record eliminates even the slightest basis for such a pretense. The cynical posturing may well help to trap us in a course of action that will prove not merely destructive but catastrophic.

Sincerely,

Noam

Postscript to Postscript, Dec. 1992:

"I am first of all of a World War II generation that was taught to take international law seriously…[In the Fletcher School of Law and Diplomacy] I studied under Leo Gross and accepted the judgement that international legal order was central to American foreign policy and had always been. In the years that followed I had no reason to think otherwise. As ambassador to India, for example, I never set foot in Goa. The United States did not recognize title to territory acquired by force. That is what the United Nations Charter was all about. Like it or not, it was law." (Senator Daniel Patrick Moynihan, letter, *National Interest*, Winter 1992/93.)

I give up.

Postscript to Postscript to Postscript

January, 1993

I didn't give up. A brief update, for some further insight into the workings of a free society. On January 17, 1993, the *New York Times Week in Review* ran a major article on the famed New World Order by Craig Whitney, under the heading "More Than Ever, U.N. Policing Is an American Show." It is devoted to the inadequacies of the UN, though Whitney, a fair and judicious man, ends by noting that "the failures of the United Nations" cannot be attributed solely to its executive: "they are the failures of the entire world community. And they will not be rectified without strong leadership from the United States." How fortunate for the world that at least one member of the "world community" is willing to stand up for principle.

Whitney's article opens with the historical background:

> Since it was established after World War II, the United Nations has been only as effective as its most powerful member states allowed it to be. The Soviet Union, for most of its history, opposed the United States in the Security

Council and in almost all cases blocked the United Nations from meaningful action. In those instances where the United Nations was able to act, from Korea to the Persian Gulf, it always did so with the strong political backing and the military muscle of the United States.

The picture is entirely accurate up to the 1950s, when US power was so extraordinary that it could use the UN as an instrument of its foreign policy, directed against the Soviet Union and other enemies. By the 1960s, the situation was radically different. Turning to the more relevant past two decades, from 1970 through 1990 the US vetoed 47 Security Council resolutions alone, 11 others with the UK, four with the UK and France. Britain had 26 negative votes (11 with the US, 4 with the US and France). France had 11 (7 alone) and the USSR 8 (one with China). Thus 80 of the 88 vetoes were by the West, 73 of them by the Anglo-Saxon defenders of the UN, 62 by the US. In the General Assembly, US isolation was even more striking. US undermining of the UN would have been even more dramatic, were it not for the fact that its enormous power kept major issues from the UN agenda. The Soviet invasion of Afghanistan was bitterly and repeatedly censured, but the UN was never willing to be destroyed by addressing the US wars in Indochina. I put aside the assault against the UN by the Reaganites, who punished the organization by withholding payments and pushing it to the verge of bankruptcy, virtually destroying UNESCO because of its Third World orientation, undermining UN human rights activities because they were annoying such friends as Argentine and Salvadoran torturers, and so on. Furthermore, this contempt for the UN continued right through the Gulf War, though concealed by the media; see my article in *Collateral Damage,* cited above.

Whitney's last sentence, however, at least approaches accuracy, though to understand it, we must again translate from *Times*-speak to English: Given the contempt of the Enforcer for international law, the UN was able to "act" to endorse (or at least not openly oppose) military and other actions that Washington was planning to undertake for its own interests. That aside, the UN could act only with great power approval, the US having the decisive voice, given the power relations.

It would be unfair to suggest that the US media are alone in this revealing manifestation of the deeply totalitarian strains of the intellectual culture. Looking north, the lead editorial in the *Toronto Globe & Mail* (Jan. 7, 1993) deals with the now fashionable topic of "humanitarian" intervention under the heading "The UN's mandate to intervene." The editors explain that the UN's founders assumed that consensus among the great powers would permit intervention to protect people from state terror and other horrors, but "they had not counted on the Cold War, which paralyzed the Council as Washington and Moscow (especially Moscow) used their veto power to block any UN action they found inconvenient" (my emphasis). Now, at last, we understand why there was no "humanitarian intervention" in El Salvador, Guatemala, South America under the neo-Nazi Generals, Indonesia when Suharto oversaw the slaughter of hundreds of thousands to the unrestrained applause of US observers, South Africa and Rhodesia, Israel's occupied territories, and on, and on.

Notes

1. Traub, *NYT Magazine*, Sept. 16, 1990.
2. Elaine Sciolino, *NYT*, Aug. 28, 1990.
3. *NYT*, Jan. 28, 1976.
4. *A Dangerous Place* (Little Brown, 1978).
5. Carmel Budiardjo, letter, *Manchester Guardian Weekly*, Sept. 30, 1990.
6. *NYT*, Sept. 24, 1990.
7. Editorial, *NYT*, Oct. 2, 1990. On the diplomatic record, the media cover-up, and its consequences, see *Deterring Democracy*, chap. 6, "Afterword."
8. *NYT Week in Review*, Sept. 23.
9. Editorial, *BG*, Oct. 7, 1990.
10. "Nightline," *BG*, Sept. 23, 1990.

10

Our "Sense of Moral Purpose"

December 10, 1990

Dear *LOOT,*

On December 7, in celebration of "the date which will live in infamy," the Bush Administration announced "that it would rush $48.1 million in military aid to the Government of El Salvador," exhibiting again the "sense of moral purpose" that so entrances the cheerleaders.[1] The aid is largely drawn from 1991 appropriations, which means that Congress may soon be pressured to provide new funding to maintain the projected 1991 level. In the background lies the October 19 congressional vote to withhold 50 percent of planned military aid in protest against the government's failure to investigate or prosecute those responsible for the assassination of six leading Jesuit intellectuals a year earlier (November 1989) by a US-trained elite battalion. As the new aid was announced on December 7, the Salvadoran Judge closed the investigation into the assassination. Archbishop Arturo Rivera y Damas told reporters that his decision meant that the "masterminds" were now free from punishment.[2]

It is evident with no further comment that US aid can only shift the balance in favor of the rulers it has chosen for El Salvador, assuring their dominance over what remains of the country, in continued service to the foreign master.

The *Times* report on the accelerated aid is confined to Administration propaganda, with no attempt at evaluation. The White House decision is presented as a response to a guerrilla offensive with new and more advanced weapons, which "almost surely come from either Cuba or Nicaragua or both," a State Department official says, though "hard evidence" is still lacking; the story, repeated two days later by Lindsey Gruson, has a familiar ring. The "overall picture," the same official adds, "remains one of a movement toward democracy and an end to conflicts," but the Salvadoran rebels "have found it a little difficult to adjust to reality."

The "overall picture" portrays reality as understood by the US government and the *New York Times*. But, merely out of idle curiosity, one might want to inquire further. How does the FMLN perceive reality? Why is it conducting an offensive, and what is the source of its arms? What do the Jesuits who survived have to say about these matters, and how do other Salvadorans view them? Those who might be curious about such questions will have to look elsewhere.

The factual content of the *Times* report has to do with the accelerated aid. Even on this narrow point, there is an intriguing tale, well concealed. In October, Congress voted to hold back $42.5 in military aid to El Salvador. The Administration objected, but not too vociferously. Why should this have been so?

A possible answer is provided by the respected Guatemalan *Central America Report*.[3] It reports that on August 27 the International Monetary Fund (IMF) had approved a loan of $50 million to El Salvador. The joint effect of the decisions by Congress and the IMF was therefore to increase aid to El Salvador; the new funding increases the level again. This was the first IMF loan since July 1982, when US funding for its terror state moved into high gear. As Congress voted to restrict the funding, the IMF (which is largely under US influence and control) expeditiously moved back in.

Theoretically, the IMF is providing "economic aid," but that never causes problems when the boss chooses to look the other way. The IMF loan to El Salvador would be hard to justify under IMF technical criteria. Under Reagan administration pressures, however, the organization (like others) was hopelessly politicized, losing what credibility it had as an independent agency pursuing the economic agenda of the rich industrial powers in terms of strictly "economic" criteria (themselves hardly neutral, but that is a different matter).

More information appears in an important November 7 release of the Center for International Policy in Washington, distributed to the media, to no avail. The Center was able to obtain IMF staff reports and adds other information about the August IMF decision and its significance. On May 3, President Cristiani had announced that any economic aid would be reallocated as necessary "for defense purposes"; economic aid is military aid. On October 13, with the congressional vote pending, Cristiani's Defense Minister Colonel Ponce announced that "the government will seek alternative means of financing the military so as not to affect the military budget, and thus the Armed Forces' actions." Ponce did not add that such "alternative means" had already been provided by Washington's dirty tricks department.

The August IMF grant, of which $32 million has already been disbursed, springs loose other funds, the Center report continues. In September, El Salvador was granted a debt-rescheduling agreement worth over $100 million, amounting to another loan. The IMF says that apart from its own aid (the largest component of which is provided by the US taxpayer) and the bilateral arrangements of the US and its allies, another $60 million is expected from multilateral sources in 1990, increasing to $100 million in 1991, along with a World Bank loan of $40 million. European Community loans are linked to advances in peace negotiations; the IMF, under US domination, is free from this impediment.

US actions are also free from the impediment of exposure. I have found no reference to any of this, apart from a mention in the last paragraph of a *Boston Globe* news report.[4] The US clients are therefore free to continue their grim work to construct the proper reality and impose "democracy," Washington-style.

An independent press would also pursue the other questions raised; vigorously, in the light of the abysmal US record in the region. Given our show of anguish over the assassination of the Jesuits, we might begin with them—noting, incidentally, that what the murdered Jesuits themselves had to say, which is most informative, has been kept from the US audience. These were Jesuit *intellectuals*, it will be recalled; the best way to bury them forever is to suppress their words, as has been done with impressive efficiency by the journals and commentators who profess to agonize over their fate, as the interested reader can easily determine.

The survivors are accorded pretty much the same treatment. The Jesuit journal *Proceso*, published by the university (UCA) where the priests were murdered, condemns the "gigantic and infamous web of complicity" that blocks the investigation of the massacre, "entrenched in the desks of the Ministry and Vice-Ministries of Defense and behind the walls of the US Embassy." It reviews evidence of "the conspiracy of silence and cover-up," which has "now landed on the doorstep of the State Department." Commenting on the congressional aid cut, the journal observes that "the Bush Administration can manipulate and even violate at its discretion the conditions contained in the [congressional vote] and/or continue to use its vast resources to keep providing military support to the Salvadoran government"—exactly as it has done. It alleges further that "the Bush Administration has sent over $100 million in military aid to El Salvador over the past ten months in unspent funds appropriated during previous years," citing evidence that $50 million of such funds was provided from August through November.[5]

Here we have further leads for enterprising news bureaus. If correct, these reports indicate that while the cover-up of the assassination was underway, steps were being taken to ensure that any emotional reactions to these atrocities would be ineffectual.

I stress *these atrocities*. Labor leaders, human rights activists, students, peasants, and other low-life are fair game and their slaughter and torture leads to no calls for reduction of aid. But the Salvadoran Jesuits, in their back-wardness, fail to comprehend the norms of civilized society. At a Mass in San Salvador commemorating the assassination (unreported to my knowledge), the Central American head of the Jesuit order, Rev. Jose Maria Tojeira, said that "The developed world's solidarity will not be authentic as long as it is limited to supporting us, the Jesuits,… while alienation, poverty and injustice continue to batter the dis-enfranchised."[6]

Could there be a message here?

It would also not be entirely impossible to unearth the FMLN conception of reality, as expressed, for example, in their "Proclamation to the Nation" of September 24, 1990, calling for "the end of militarism, a new social and eco-nomic order, the democratization of the nation and the restoration of our sovereignty and an independent foreign policy"—all spelled out in some detail. Nor would it be a hopeless task to discover the published records of the Na-tional Debate for Peace, which has brought together under Church auspices virtually all organized groups in the coun-try. These records tell us much about how Salvadorans see reality. The participants, from a broad range of social sec-tors, express near unanimous condemnation of "the enor-mous interference of the U.S. in El Salvador's national affairs," of US military aid in any form, of military interfer-ence in state and society "in support of the oligarchy and dominant sectors, and thus in support of North American interests" as the country is "subjugated to the interests of international capital," and so on. The concern for our little brown brothers is attested by the attention showered on this illuminating study, readily available in Washington, but scrupulously barred from the Free Press.[7]

The *Central America Report* provides further informa-tion on the questions left unexplored. The government of Costa Rica reported an increase in arms shipments entering the country through summer 1990: "Most of the weapons are believed to originate from contra stockpiles not handed

over to the UN and destined for Colombia and El Salvador."
The journal also reported an inquiry of the Socialist International into the assassination of Salvadoran socialist leader
Hector Oqueli and Guatemalan lawyer Hilda Flores in Guatemala on January 12, 1990. The inquiry, conducted by Professors Tom Farer and Robert Goldman of American
University, concluded that they were probably murdered by
the Salvadoran right, perhaps in an effort to undermine
peace negotiations. Mexico's leading daily reports further
that President Cristiani's intelligence services are now operating in Nicaragua, "as confirmed by the recent raid and
search of the offices of a Salvadoran refugee religious organization in Managua," the Ecclesiastical Ecumenical and Service Base Communities, by armed men, some in uniform.[8]

These are further examples of reality, as the US extends "democracy" through the region.

One of the crimes of the Sandinistas was that they
allowed Nicaragua to become a refuge for writers, human
rights activists, priests, peasants and others who escaped
from the death squad democracies, much as France offered
sanctuary to victims of fascist terror half a century ago. It is
safe to assume that the US will seek to overcome such
failures to "adjust to reality."

Other crimes committed in the region have yet to be
rectified completely. The US terror operations were set in
motion as popular organizations began to take root, in part
inspired by the "preferential option for the poor" adopted
by segments of the Church. While US terror has largely
succeeded in restoring the traditional and more satisfactory
preferential option for the rich, there still remain unwelcome residues of these and other efforts, posing a continued
threat of democracy and justice. In Nicaragua, the UNO
government has not proven fully obedient, or sufficiently
harsh and brutal for US tastes; nor has it yet recognized
adequately the priorities of traditional wealth, including returning exiles, Somozists and others of the traditional
wealthy classes. And despite US pressures—among them,

withholding of the trickle of promised aid—the UNO government has not abandoned the World Court case and its call for reparations for the huge disaster inflicted by the United States in the course of its "unlawful use of force" and illegal economic warfare of the past decade. The US of course has no intention of adhering to the judgment of the World Court, but the lingering annoyance is a bit of an embarrassment amidst the current posturing about the sanctity of international law. There is, then, much to be done.[9]

It is likely that it is being done. The eyes of the public are focused on the Gulf, but the state has many eyes, and many busy hands, and the present moment is an opportune one to pursue its goals without fear of exposure (minimal at best). The El Salvador shenanigans are a case in point. There is also circumstantial evidence that clandestine operations may be underway in Nicaragua to remove the Chamorro government in favor of more obedient and vicious clients, who will also return the security forces to US control, as the Carter Administration vainly tried to ensure in 1979 after its ally Somoza could no longer be sustained. It has been a leading principle of US policy since early postwar days, spelled out in the internal planning record and consistently pursued in practice, that the means of violence must be in the hands of the US and its clients so that any failure to "adjust to reality" will be properly terminated. Perhaps a decade hence, some enterprising journalist will discover that there is more than a little truth to the statements of President Violeta Chamorro and Interior Minister Carlos Hurtado that "dark forces" are manipulating the current unrest and disorder—not merely Virgilio Godoy as the scant reporting here assumes, but more traditional and powerful forces.[10]

Sincerely,

Noam

LOOT, 2.1, January 1991

Notes

1. Clifford Krauss, *New York Times*, Dec. 8, 1990. See Thomas Friedman, cited in letter 9.

2. AP, *Boston Globe*, Dec. 10, 1990, World Briefs; ignored in the *New York Times*.

3. *CAR*, Sept. 21, 1990.

4. Pamela Constable, "Jesuit case has sharpened US dilemma in Salvador," *BG*, Nov. 18, 1990.

5. Editorials, *Proceso*, Oct. 31, Nov. 7, 1990.

6. AP, Nov. 17, 1990.

7. see *Necessary Illusions*, 243f.

8. *CAR*, Oct. 5, 26; *Excelsior*, Nov. 5, 1990.

9. See letter 15, on US success in compelling Nicaragua to withdraw the claims validated by the World Court, and the sequel.

10. AP, *BG*, Nov. 16, 1990. On the longstanding doctrine that security forces must be under unilateral US control, see my *On Power and Ideology* (South End, 1987), lecture 1; *Year 501*, chap. 7.3.

11
"We the People"

Dear *LOOT*,

As voters—a few of them at least—went to the polls on November 6, the *New York Times* featured two front-page stories on the elections.

In the first, Michael Oreskes reports that "Everyone agreed it had been one of the weirdest midterm election seasons of modern times…with restless voters looking for ways to lash out at politicians and worried about war in the Persian Gulf and recession here at home." The sub-head reads: "Low Turnout Expected"; "Public is Swept by 2 Tides—Desire for Change and Fear of War and a Recession." The mood of the voters is one of frustration and anger at government and the whole political system.

The second article, by R.W. Apple, is headlined "War Clouds, No Thunder; With the Guns Silent, So Are the Candidates." Apple opens by noting that "Two years ago, a Presidential campaign took place at a time of radical change in the world order, with the Soviet Union rapidly ceasing to pose a threat to the West, and there was almost no debate about what the United States should do. This year, a midterm election campaign has taken place with war threatening in the Persian Gulf, and once again the major foreign policy issue confronting the nation has generated almost no debate about what the United States should do." In short, as in the past, the political campaign avoided the most important issues facing the country: war and recession, the former perhaps the most ominous crisis since World War II. The United States was heading into a war, virtually isolated apart from England, with consequences that could be catastrophic. But it was not an issue in the political campaign, a replay of the pattern of the past.

In his front-page wrap-up article on the elections, Apple observed that "only a third of those eligible to do so even bothered to cast ballots" and the voters, "unhappy with politics as usual," expressed antagonism to government—insofar as choices were open to them at all.[1] He did not address the reasons for the (characteristic) avoidance of policy issues and the limited choices available to voters, or the media's role in perpetuating these conditions.

The two lead election-day stories suggest a certain hypothesis: There is a relationship between the two issues that were addressed, between the mood of frustration and anger, on the one hand, and the avoidance of the crucial issues by the candidates, on the other. A reasonable hypothesis might be that popular anger reflects the failure of the political system to function; people are angry because they are granted no voice on issues of major importance to them. A look at American political history, particularly in recent years, supports that hypothesis. The public has become more and more alienated from the political system, and more cynical about other institutions as well, while activism outside of formal political channels has been on the rise through the '70s and '80s. Major issues are excluded from the arena of electoral choice, from political debate, and from the political culture generally, which keeps to a very narrow spectrum of tactical judgments among elite preferences. That is the "big story" about the 1990 elections, and those that came before.

As should be a commonplace, there is essentially one political party, the business party, with two factions. Shifting coalitions of investors account for a large part of political history. Unions or other popular organizations that might offer a way for the general public to play some role in developing programs and influencing policy choices scarcely function. The ideological system is bounded by the consensus of the privileged. In congressional elections, virtually all incumbents are returned to office. There is scarcely a pretense that substantive issues arise in presidential campaigns. Articulated programs are hardly more than a device to garner votes, and it is considered quite natural for candidates to adjust messages to audiences as public relations tacticians advise, another reflection of the vacuity of the political system and the cynicism of those who participate in it. Political commentators ponder such questions as whether Reagan will remember his lines, or whether Mondale looks too gloomy, or whether Dukakis can duck the slime flung at him by George Bush's speech writers. In the 1984 elections, the two factions virtually exchanged traditional stands, the Republicans presenting themselves as the party of Keynesian growth and state intervention in the economy, the Democrats as the advocates of fiscal conservatism; few even noticed. Half the population does not bother to push the levers, and those who take the trouble often consciously vote against their own interest.

The public is granted an opportunity to ratify decisions made elsewhere. It may select among personalities put forth in a game of symbolic politics that only the most naive take very seriously. When they do, they are mocked by sophisticates. Criticism of President Bush's call for "revenue enhancement" after having won the election by the eloquent promise not to raise taxes is a "political cheap shot," Harvard political scientist and media specialist Marty Linsky comments under the heading "Campaign pledges—made to be broken." When Bush led the public in his "read my lips—no new taxes" chant, he was merely expressing his "world view," making "a statement of his hopes." Those who thought he was promising no new taxes do not understand that "elections and governing are different ball games, played with different objectives and rules." "The purpose of elections is to win," Linsky correctly observes, expressing the profound elite contempt for democracy; and "the purpose of governing is to do the best for the country," he adds, parroting the illusions that respectability demands.[2]

These deeply anti-democratic tendencies were accelerated during the Reagan years. The population largely opposed the policies of his administration; exit polls in 1984
showed that voters, by about 3 to 2, hoped that his legisla-
tive program would not be enacted. In the 1980 elections, 4
percent of the electorate voted for Reagan because they
regarded him as a "real conservative." In 1984, the percent-
age dropped to 1 percent. That is what is called "a landslide
victory for conservatism" in political rhetoric. Furthermore,
contrary to much pretense, Reagan's popularity was never
particularly high, and much of the population seemed to
understand that he was a media creation, who had only the
foggiest idea of what government policy might be.[3]

It is noteworthy that the fact is now tacitly conceded;
the instant that the "great communicator" was no longer of
any use as a symbol, the media quietly tucked him away.
After eight years of pretense about the "revolution" that
Reagan wrought, no one would dream of asking its standard bearer for his thoughts about any topic, because it is
understood, as it always was, that he has none. When
Reagan was invited to Japan as an elder statesman, his hosts
were surprised—and given the fat fee, a bit annoyed—to
discover that he could not hold press conferences or talk on
any subject. Their discomfiture aroused some amusement
in the US press: the Japanese believed what the media here
had reported about this remarkable figure, failing to comprehend the workings of the mysterious occidental mind.

The hoax perpetrated by the media and the intellectual community is of some general interest. State capitalist
democracy has a certain tension with regard to the locus of
power: in principle, the people rule, but effective power
resides largely in private hands, with large-scale effects
throughout the social order. One way to reduce the tension
is to remove the public from the scene, except in form. The
Reagan phenomenon offered a new way to achieve this
fundamental goal of capitalist democracy. The office of
chief executive was, in effect, eliminated in favor of a sym-

bolic figure constructed by the public relations industry to perform certain ritual tasks: to appear on ceremonial occasions, to greet visitors, read government pronouncements, and so on. While Reagan is often described as the US counterpart of Margaret Thatcher, a better analogue would be the Queen, who also performs such functions, even opening Parliament by reading the government's program. No one asks whether she believes it, or even understands it. The same was true of the "great communicator," a fact that had to be carefully concealed for 8 years, though now pretense can be dropped—though true loyalists, like *Wall Street Journal* editors, hang on grimly.

Reducing elections to the level of choice of acting Queen is a major advance in the marginalization of the public. As the most sophisticated of the state capitalist democracies, the United States has often led the way in devising means to control the domestic enemy, and the latest inspiration will doubtless be replayed here when the appropriate moment comes, and mimicked elsewhere, with the usual lag.

These tendencies are quite in accord with the concept of democracy that has long been espoused by leading democratic theorists, a concept that helps explain the institutional role of the media. From the first modern democratic revolution in England in the 17th century, it has been a common theme of intellectual discourse that means must be found to ensure that the "rascal multitude" do not interfere with serious matters.[4] The dean of modern American journalism, Walter Lippmann, was also a highly respected progressive democratic theorist, and articulated the basic ideas as clearly as anyone. "The public must be put in its place," he wrote, so that we may "live free of the trampling and the roar of a bewildered herd." If they cannot be subdued by force, then their thoughts must be efficiently controlled; lacking coercive force, authority can only turn to indoctrination to achieve the essential ends. So-called "conservatives" are only more extreme in their dedication to taming the despised rabble. Elaborating further, Lippmann distinguished two political roles within a modern democracy. First, there is the role assigned to the "specialized class," the "insiders," the "responsible men," who have access to information and understanding. These "public men" are responsible for "the formation of a sound public opinion." "They initiate, they administer, they settle," and should be protected from "ignorant and meddlesome outsiders," the general public, who lack the competence to deal "with the substance of the problem." The specialized class, protected from meddlesome outsiders, will serve what is called "the national interest" in the webs of mystification spun by the academic social sciences and political commentary.

There is, to be sure, an unspoken premise. The "public men" gain access to authority and become "experts" insofar as they serve the interests of private power. Lippmann was a "responsible man" while Eugene Debs was in jail; the distinction reflects nothing more than their different commitments and values. These trivial truths, which would be discussed in elementary school in a free society, must be suppressed—and if heard by some accident, angrily denied—or too much of reality becomes exposed to view. It is best that the "public men" themselves be immune from any self-understanding, so that they may better carry out their responsibilities—and keep their jobs.

The first role to be filled in a properly functioning democracy, then, is that of the "responsible men": to manage public affairs in the interests of private power ("the national interest"). The second role is that of the public, which is far more limited. It is not "the task of the public," Lippmann observes, to "pass judgment on the intrinsic merits" of an issue or to offer analysis or solutions, but merely, on occasion, to place "its force at the disposal" of one or another group of "responsible men" in what are called "elections." The public "does not reason, investigate, invent, persuade, bargain or settle." Rather, "the public acts only by aligning itself as the partisan of someone in a position to act executively," once he has given the matter at hand sober and disinterested thought. The bewildered herd, trampling and roaring, "has its function": to be "the interested spectators of action," not participants. Participation is the duty of "the responsible men," who know how to follow orders.

To serve these ends is a solemn obligation. It is thus unfair to criticize those who help to divert and control the public mind, thus protecting our democratic system from the ignorant rabble who might subvert it by trying to meddle in affairs that are none of their business. Our fabled "yearning for democracy" demands no less.

When the press features this story, we will know that it has become an instrument of enlightenment, not indoctrination. But no such insubordination can seriously be contemplated without far broader moves towards realizing democratic and libertarian ideals that would truly subvert existing structures of power and domination.

Sincerely,

Noam

LOOT, 2.3, March 1991

Notes

1. Apple, *NYT*, Nov. 8, 1990.
2. Linsky, *Boston Globe*, July 7, 1990.
3. 1992 polls found Reagan to be the most unpopular living ex-President apart from Nixon, who he beat by a shade (58 percent popularity to Nixon's 54 percent). Highest was Carter (74 percent), second Ford (68 percent), largely because he is unknown, one might guess. Reagan is particularly disliked by working people and "Reagan Democrats," who gave him "the highest unfavorable rating [63 percent] of a wide range of public officials," one study found. See *Year 501,* chap. 11.1.
4. For discussion, see *Deterring Democracy*, chap. 12.

12
Bringing Peace

April 12, 1991

Dear *LOOT*,

"When this war is over," George Bush announced in January, "the United States, its credibility and its reliability restored, will have a key leadership role in helping to bring peace to the rest of the Middle East." With the war over, James Baker flew at once to the region, meeting with Israel and the Arab allies: the six family dictatorships that manage Gulf oil production, the bloody tyrant who rules Syria, and Egypt. In a "watershed event," they "endorsed President Bush's broad framework for dealing with the Middle East," chief diplomatic correspondent Thomas Friedman gushed.[1]

Even critics were impressed. Anthony Lewis wrote that the President is "at the height of his powers" and "has made very clear that he wants to breathe light into that hypothetical creature, the Middle East peace process." Helena Cobban found "great inspiration" in Bush's statement that "The time has come to put an end to the Arab-Israeli conflict," words "spoken with commitment by an American president at the height of his powers" and forming part of his "broad vision of Middle East peace-building." John Judis praised Secretary of State James Baker as the hope for peace, a dove who "has stood for multilateral and diplomatic solutions" and has "emphasized that the U.S. would have to work on resolving the conflict between Israel and the Palestinians."[2]

The *New York Times* editors saw "a rare window for peace." "The P.L.O's Iraqi debacle...could bring forward acceptable negotiating partners" among the Palestinians, permitting "direct bargaining between Israel and representative Palestinians"—"representative" being a code word for "acceptable to us." Adopting the same Orwellisms, the *Washington Post* editors agreed that talks between Israel and the Arab states were preferable to an "unprepared and unwieldy international conference," and offer "the best way to make sure that the Palestinians, once they locate representative and plausible spokesmen, will receive their regional due." The *Wall Street Journal* announced that although "Bush Hopes for a Solution," "the PLO's Leaders Must Want One as Well."[3]

A few weeks earlier, the editors of the *Los Angeles Times* had admonished the Palestinians that they "will have to do better than" Yasser Arafat, even if he is "their sincere choice." They must abandon the "leadership that has habitually opted for no-compromise dogmatism at the expense of conciliation, frequently using assassination to silence moderate opposition voices within Palestinian ranks." The next day, Israel arrested yet another leading Arab advocate of Palestinian-Arab dialogue, Dr. Mamdouh al-Aker, subjecting him to torture as usual and keeping him from his attorney for a month—the real story about "moderate opposition voices" for many years, regularly suppressed in favor of convenient fictions, such as the "no-compromise dogmatism" of those who for many years have been far closer to the international consensus on a political settlement than the Washington-media rejectionist alliance.[4]

It did not pass without notice that a few problems remained. After hailing the "watershed event," Thomas Friedman added that "The Arab ministers clearly differed with Mr. Baker on one very important detail: how to make peace with Israel." They called for "an international conference under the auspices of the United Nations" while "Mr. Baker, by contrast, said an international conference would not be appropriate at this time." "On secondary issues, such as the Palestinian-Israeli dispute, [the Arab states] still prefer the safety of the Arab lowest common denominator—at least for now." The issue is "secondary" by virtue of Washington's orders and Israel's preference.

The official Arab statement after the "watershed event" reveals another "detail," recorded without comment: The Arab allies "demand the full and unconditional implementation of Security Council Resolution 425" of March 1978, the first of several calling for Israel's immediate and unconditional withdrawal from Lebanon. The plea was renewed by the government of Lebanon in February 1991, ignored as usual while Israel and its clients terrorize the occupied southern region and bomb elsewhere at will.[5]

In the real world, the Arab allies have some company in calling for an international conference. Consider the United Nations. Since January 1976, the Security Council has been rendered "utterly ineffective" by the US veto (to borrow the words of the revered exponent of international law who cast the veto, in that crucial case). But the matter arises regularly in the General Assembly, including the latest annual session (December 1990), when the call for such a conference passed 144-2 (US and Israel opposing). In the preceding session, the Assembly had voted 151-3 (US, Israel, Dominica) for an international conference to realize the terms of UN Resolution 242, along with "the right to self-determination" for the Palestinians.[6] These resolutions recapitulate the proposals of the Arab states and the PLO in January 1976. Europe, the USSR, the Arab states and the PLO, and the world generally have been united for years on such a political settlement. But the US will not permit it. These facts being quite unacceptable, they are eliminated from history.[7]

For twenty years, the US has backed Israeli rejectionism. Therefore the peace process remains a "hypothetical creature," a truth that is improper, therefore inexpressible. An international conference is unacceptable to the US, in the first place, because participants will support "the right to self-determination" for the indigenous population. An even more fundamental reason is that there will be participants. This feature of an international conference violates the basic precept that the Middle East is US turf, the Monroe

Doctrine having been extended to the world's major energy resources after World War II. For such simple and sufficient reasons, an international conference is "unwieldy" and "inappropriate."

Many reporters and editors may be unaware of the basic facts, being limited to US coverage; it is hard to imagine that Thomas Friedman shares this highly convenient ignorance—particularly, given his record in suppressing the facts, surely consciously, during his service as Jerusalem correspondent.[8]

Friedman observed further that Washington is exploring the idea of peace talks with "a ceremonial opening 'event'" hosted by the US and USSR. Israeli Prime Minister Yitzhak Shamir would find this preferable to an "open-ended, gang-up-on-Israel international conference."[9] John Judis detected Baker's benign hand in this move towards peace.

In the real world, Washington is willing to allow the Soviet Union to co-host a ceremonial "event" on the assumption that in its current straits, it will follow orders. But as Kissinger warned years ago, Europe and Japan must be kept out of the diplomacy; they are too independent (Britain aside). The President of the European Community and its official in charge of Middle East affairs recently reiterated the EC position expressed in regular UN Resolutions, declaring that "The outside powers should not let Israel get off the hook once again"; Israel should withdraw from Lebanon and the occupied territories, and reach a settlement with Syria on the Syrian Golan Heights (annexed in defiance of a Security Council resolution and a General Assembly vote of 149-1). But, they added, the EC would play no further serious role in the diplomatic process, now recognized, at last, to be a US monopoly.[10]

In their own quaint way, the media acknowledge these realities. The *New York Times* has mentioned that the US is alone in the world in endorsing Israel's Shamir plan (Joel Brinkley). But "the Soviet Union has moved away from a policy of confrontation with the United States and now indicates that it prefers partnership with Washington in the diplomacy of the region," *Times* Middle East correspondent Alan Cowell later added hopefully under the headline "Soviets Trying to Become Team Player in Mideast." This "shift away from confrontation" brings the Soviet Union "closer to the mainstream of Mideast diplomacy," he explained.[11]

To translate from *Times*-speak, the Soviet Union may join Washington in its splendid isolation, thereby becoming a "team player" in "the mainstream." "The team" is the United States, "the mainstream" is the position occupied by "the team," and the "peace process" is whatever "the team" is doing. Period.

Since late 1989, the official "peace process" has been the Baker plan, which, as Baker announced loud and clear, is identical to the Shamir plan; more accurately, the Peres-Shamir plan, the coalition plan of Israel's two major political blocs, Labor and Likud. Palestinians will be limited to discussing its modalities, with the PLO excluded, Baker announced without equivocation. The current propaganda line is that when "The Palestinians supported Iraq during the gulf war and endorsed its missile attacks on Israel, Mr. Baker's response was to freeze the Palestine Liberation Organization out of his talks" (Friedman).[12] As Friedman surely knows, all of Baker's conditions were explicit as official policy long before the Gulf war—in fact, in fall 1989, at just the time that Baker was exerting every effort to ensure that aid would flow to Saddam Hussein.[13]

The Baker-Shamir-Peres plan had three "Basic Premises." First, there can be no "additional Palestinian state," Jordan already being one; there is no issue of Palestinian self-determination, whatever the foolish and irresponsible world may think. Second, no PLO; Palestinians may not choose their own representatives to sign the capitulation being prepared for them. Third, "There will be no change in the status of Judea, Samaria and Gaza other than in accordance with the basic guidelines of the Government" of Israel, which rule out Palestinian national rights. The plan then calls for "free elections" under Israeli military occupation with much of the Palestinian leadership rotting in prison, sometimes without charge, sometimes after "trials" before military courts that scarcely qualify as ludicrous. The outcome, as Israeli officials have made clear, is that Palestinians may be allowed to set local tax rates in Nablus and collect garbage in Ramallah. If put forward by some state other than "the symbol of human decency," such proposals would scarcely be accorded ridicule.

Unlike US commentators, the semi-official Egyptian press finds little "inspiration" in the Bush-Baker rhetoric. Any hopes that Egypt might have had evaporated after Baker's March 1991 visit, when he underscored traditional US rejectionism.[14] There were no grounds for optimism in the first place, given that the great power that has long barred any meaningful peace process has now established that "what we say goes," as the President put it a few days after "staking out the high ground."

A central task of the "responsible men," in Lippmann's sense, is to fix clearly the bounds of opinion. At one extreme, we have Yitzhak Shamir, who holds that the "land for peace" formula of UN 242 has already been satisfied. At the other, we have the opposition Labor Party, which sees advantages for Israel in "territorial compromise" along the lines of Labor's Allon plan, leaving Israel in control of the useful land and resources but without responsibility for most of the Arab population. The US is an honest broker, merely seeking peace and justice, trying to steer a path between "the conditions the Arab nations and Israel have put on their possible participation in any peace conference," as Thomas Friedman puts it.[15] The world has long refused to "join the team," so there is no need to report its childish fancies.

One useful device is to select a few "good Arabs" to whom one can attribute positions held by the Washington-media alliance, truth having its usual significance. Thus in

Friedman's version of history, in Jerusalem in 1977 President Sadat "offered the Israeli people full peace in return for a full withdrawal from the Sinai desert." As Friedman of course knows, that was Menachem Begin's position, while Sadat sharply disagreed; he clearly and explicitly reiterated the international consensus, calling for the establishment of a Palestinian state in the West Bank and Gaza as proposed in the Security Council resolution of January 1976 that the US had vetoed. Continuing, Friedman writes that now "The Arab countries have been demanding that Israel commit itself to an interpretation of 242 that leaves open the possibility of trading land for peace." As he again knows, the Arab countries *reject* this US-Israeli formula, joining the world in an interpretation of 242 that calls for political settlement on the internationally recognized (pre-June 1967) border, with perhaps minor and mutual adjustments—official US policy as well, before Kissinger took control in 1971.[16]

Palestinians and authentic Israeli doves have commonly regarded the Labor-US "territorial compromise" variety of rejectionism as "much worse than the Likud's autonomy plan" (Shmuel Toledano, endorsing the observation of Palestinian moderate Attorney Aziz Shehadah).[17] The reasons are well-known, but must remain as deeply buried as the actual history.

Washington's rejectionist stance must be adopted as the basis for reporting and discussion, while its advocates are lauded as doves who intend to breathe light on the problems of suffering humanity; these are the conditions of "responsible discourse." The US and Israel can then proceed with the policy articulated in February 1989 by Defense Secretary Yitzhak Rabin of the Labor Party, when he informed Peace Now leaders that the US-PLO dialogue was only a means to divert attention while Israel suppresses the Intifada by force. The Palestinians "will be broken," he assured them, reiterating the prediction of Israeli Arabists 40 years earlier: the Palestinians will "be crushed," will die or "turn into human dust and the waste of society, and join the most impoverished classes in the Arab countries." Or they will leave, while Russian Jews, now barred from the US by policies designed to deny them a free choice, flock to an expanded Israel, leaving the diplomatic issues moot, as the Baker-Shamir-Peres plan envisions.

New excuses will be devised for old policies, which will be hailed as generous and forthcoming. Failure will be attributed to the "no-compromise dogmatism" of the extremists who fail to adapt to Washington's "broad framework for dealing with the Middle East," which is by definition right and just. As long as the public is unaware and silent, it remains only to watch the ugly scenario unfold.

Sincerely,

Noam

LOOT, 2.5, May 1991

Notes

1. Andrew Rosenthal, "Bush Vows to Tackle Middle East Issues," *NYT*, Jan. 29; Friedman, *NYT*, March 11, 1991.
2. Lewis, *NYT*, March 15; Cobban, *Christian Science Monitor*, March 12; Judis, *In These Times*, Feb. 27, 1991.
3. Editorial, *NYT*, March 11; editorial, *WP weekly*, March 11-17; *WSJ*, front-page headline, March 6, 1991.
4. Editorial, *LAT*, Feb. 26, 1991. *Mideast Mirror* (London), 27 March, 1991.
5. Excerpts of Arab statement, *NYT*, March 12, 1991. On US-Israel and Lebanon, see letter 7.
6. UN Draft A/44/L.51, 6 Dec. 1989.
7. See letter 1 and sources cited; letter 9 on the US Ambassador who had such success in undermining the UN peacekeeping role.
8. See *Necessary Illusions*, 290-95.
9. *NYT*, March 28, 1991.
10. Jacques Poos, Eberhard Rhein, *Mideast Mirror*, 28 March, 1991.

11. Brinkley, *NYT,* Sept. 8; Cowell, *NYT,* Dec. 12, 1989.

12. *NYT,* April 14, "Week in Review," 1, April 14, 1991. For documentation and further detail and background, see references of letter 1, note 4.

13. See letter 2. Though much was known (and largely suppressed) about US support for Iraq at once, its extent, and Baker's crucial role in implementing it, were revealed only a few weeks after this "Letter from Lexington" was written. The story reached the US mainstream in early 1992. See Alan Friedman and Lionel Barber, *Financial Times* (London), May 3, May 24; AP, *BG,* May 23; Ralph Atkins et al., *FT,* July 29; James Adams and Nick Rufford, *Sunday Times* (London), July 28, 1991. On Friedman's explanation of the reasons for supporting Saddam Hussein, or some clone if he no longer serves, see letter 13.

14. *Al-Ahram,* cited in *Mideast Mirror,* 27 March, 1991.

15. *NYT,* April 13, 1991.

16. Friedman, *NYT,* "Week in Review," April 14; *NYT,* April 10, 1991.

17. *Ha'aretz,* March 8, 1991.

13
The Burdens of Responsibility

August 12, 1991

Dear *LOOT*,

Honest journalism is a demanding craft, but the respectable variety, a very different genre, has its burdens as well. The aftermath of the Gulf war provides many illustrations. Here is a small sample.

One essential talent is a tolerance for contradiction. Thus Patrick Tyler observes that "gaps remain in the Administration's goal of stemming the Middle East arms race, even as Washington has become the dominant arms supplier in the region."[1] Here we see the familiar conflict between facts and Truth, facts being what happens in the world, while Truth has a more august status, emanating from power itself. That the Administration's goal is to stem the Middle East arms race is Truth, established by assertion from on high. Washington's exploitation of the opportunity to sell high tech weapons is mere fact, too insignificant to undermine Truth. To adorn the point in scholarly garb, fact is merely "the abuse of reality," while Truth is "reality itself" (see letter 8).

Washington's inspiring benevolence is another Truth that totters uneasily alongside recalcitrant fact. Confronting the problem head on, Tyler writes: "Though Mr. Bush has made it plain that he will not tolerate needless suffering among Iraqi women and children, widespread disease and malnutrition have been documented in the country, but have not yet been addressed." The last phrase is a euphemism. The translation into English reads: "but the US and its British puppy dog are blocking efforts to deal with the civilian catastrophe."

The contradiction between fact and Truth would be

overcome if Mr. Bush were unaware of the vast and growing civilian suffering. Pursuing that heroic option, Tyler
reports that the embargo is "hurting the Iraqi people far
more than is perceived in Washington."[2] True, "severe malnutrition and spiraling disease" may be having a "devastating effect on the civilian population," but Mr. Bush hasn't
been told. The dilemma is now resolved: when he learns
about the effects of his sanctions, he will move resolutely to
help "Iraqi women and children," in accord with the principles that he has "made plain."

The astute reader will have noticed that the contradiction can be overcome in a different way. It is only *needless*
suffering that Our Leader will not tolerate. Utilitarian suffering is quite another thing. In the case in question, the
suffering serves a useful function: to hold the population
hostage for political ends (what is called "terrorism" when
done on a far lesser scale by some official enemy). The
suffering is therefore justified on realistic, pragmatic
grounds.

The reasoning is explained by Thomas Friedman: the
sanctions are intended to induce Iraqi generals to topple the
dictator, "and then Washington would have the best of all
worlds: an iron-fisted Iraqi junta without Saddam Hussein." In short, by punishing Iraqi women and children,
Washington will be able to restore the happy days when
Saddam's "iron fist…held Iraq together, much to the satis-
faction of the American allies Turkey and Saudi Arabia,"
not to speak of the boss in Washington, who had no problem with the means employed—indeed, went out of his
way to provide aid and support for the man with the iron
fist.[3]

It will be quite proper, then, to "have sat by and
watched a country starve for political reasons" (UNICEF's
director of public affairs Richard Reid, quoted in the Cana-
dian press). That is what will happen, Reid predicts, unless
Iraq is permitted to purchase "massive quantities of
food"—though it is already far too late for the children

under two, who have stopped growing for six or seven months because of severe malnutrition, he reports. It is also too late for the 55,000 children who had died by May 1991 (Patrick Tyler, reporting the Harvard medical team study that predicted another 170,000 child deaths by the end of the year), and for countless others in a country facing "widespread starvation," a critical shortage of drugs and a collapsing medical system, quadrupling of diarrheal diseases, outbreaks of typhoid and cholera in cities with raw sewage flowing in streets and into rivers, and the other forms of utilitarian suffering reported by the UN Secretary-General's mission.[4]

If Bush is lucky, his ex-pal may lend a helpful hand. The *Wall Street Journal* observes that Iraq's "clumsy attempt to hide nuclear-bomb-making equipment from the U.N. may be a blessing in disguise, U.S. officials say. It assures that the allies [read: US and UK] can keep economic sanctions in place to squeeze Saddam Hussein without mounting calls to end the penalties for humanitarian reasons."[5] No annoying noises, then, from the PC crowd as we joyfully "watch the country starve for political reasons."

The Bush-*Times* conception of "the best of all worlds" is not universally shared. London banker Ahmad Chalabi, a spokesman for the Iraqi democratic opposition, describes the outcome of the war as "the worst of all possible worlds" for the Iraqi people.[6] Another contradiction, but again only apparent and readily resolved. The worst of all possible worlds for the Iraqi people may well be the best of all worlds from the perspective of offices in Washington and New York. Right-thinking people may agree with Chalabi that "the tragedy in Iraq is awesome," meanwhile recognizing that the important concerns are those spelled out by the State Department spokesman at the *Times*. "Before Mr. Hussein invaded Kuwait," Friedman writes, "he was a pillar of the gulf balance of power and status quo preferred by Washington," employing his "iron fist" with our approval and generous assistance. He made a false move on August

2, 1990, "but as soon as Mr. Hussein was forced back into his shell, Washington felt he had become useful again... That is why Mr. Bush never supported the Kurdish and Shi'ite rebellions against Mr. Hussein, or for that matter any democracy movement in Iraq."[7]

That is also why the *Times*—in fact, the media generally—have scrupulously avoided the Iraqi democratic forces (though the *Wall Street Journal* deserves credit for allowing them a few openings well after the splendid triumph). These silly folk had the bad taste to oppose Washington's plans throughout; much like the Palestinians, they fail to recognize what *Times* correspondent Serge Schmemann calls "the hard realities of the region,"[8] and thus deserve their fate. They were calling for democracy in Iraq when Saddam's "iron fist" was providing Washington with "the best of all worlds." They opposed the ruinous US-UK war and urged pursuit of the diplomatic track that was barred by Washington and virtually suppressed by the media. And finally, compounding their sins, they are again calling for democracy in Iraq while Washington seeks to install some clone of Saddam Hussein, but one who understands that "what we say goes," in the President's fine words.

Speaking abroad, Chalabi observed in mid-March, 1991 that Washington "is waiting for Saddam to butcher the insurgents in the hope that he can be overthrown later by a suitable officer," an attitude rooted in the US policy of "supporting dictatorships to maintain stability." The Bush administration announced that it would continue to refuse any contact with Iraqi democratic leaders: "We felt that political meetings with them...would not be appropriate for our policy at this time," State Department spokesman Richard Boucher stated on March 14. The Department is true to its word. *Times* Middle East correspondent Alan Cowell reports that Iraqi exiles in Syria say "there has been no reply" to their letter requesting a meeting with James Baker, "and the embassy's doors remain closed to them," as in

Washington and New York.[9]

The traditional US opposition to democratic forces poses a constant challenge for the vigilant defenders of Truth. In the present case, the respectable commentator must play down the US military tactics: to create maximum long-lasting damage to the civilian society for the political end of restoring the "iron fist"; and to massacre defenseless conscripts (mostly Shi'ite and Kurdish peasants, apparently) hiding in holes in the sand or fleeing for their lives while elite units were released to do their necessary work and US forces were spared any danger of combat. Reporting from northern Iraq, American correspondent Charles Glass described how journalists watched as "Republican Guards, supported by regular army brigades, mercilessly shelled Kurdish-held areas with Katyusha multiple rocket launchers, helicopter gunships and heavy artillery," while they tuned in to listen to Stormin' Norman puffing on about how "We had destroyed the Republican Guard as a militarily effective force" and eliminated the military use of helicopters[10]—not the stuff of which heroes are fashioned, therefore finessed, though the story could not be totally ignored at home.

Striving manfully to reconcile fact with Truth, Alan Cowell attributes the failure of the rebels to the fact that "very few people outside Iraq wanted them to win." Here the concept "people" has its standard meaning in respectable journalism: "people who count." The "allied campaign against President Hussein brought the United States and its Arab coalition partners to a strikingly unanimous view," Cowell continues: "whatever the sins of the Iraqi leader, he offered the West and the region a better hope for his country's stability than did those who have suffered his repression."[11]

These "Arab coalition partners" are a merry crew: six family dictatorships, Syria's Hafez el-Assad (indistinguishable from Saddam Hussein), and Egypt, the sole Arab ally with a degree of internal freedom. We therefore look to the semi-official press in Egypt to verify Cowell's report of the "strikingly unanimous view" among "people." His article is datelined Damascus, April 10. The day before, Deputy Editor Salaheddin Hafez of Egypt's leading (and semi-official) daily, *al-Ahram*, commented on Saddam's demolition of the rebels "under the umbrella of the Western alliance's forces." The US stance proved what Egypt had been saying all along, Hafez wrote. American rhetoric about "the savage beast, Saddam Hussein," was merely a cover for the true goals: to cut Iraq down to size and establish US hegemony in the region. The West turned out to be in total agreement with the beast on the need to "block any progress and abort all hopes, however dim, for freedom or equality and for progress towards democracy," working in "collusion with Saddam himself" if necessary.[12]

There was, indeed, some regional support for the US stance. In Israel, many commentators (including leading doves) agreed with retiring Chief-of-Staff Dan Shomron that it is preferable for Saddam Hussein to remain in power in Iraq. Others welcomed the suppression of the Kurds because of "the latent ambition of Iran and Syria to exploit the Kurds and create a territorial, military, contiguity between Teheran and Damascus—a contiguity which embodies danger for Israel" (Moshe Zak). But all this was unhelpful, therefore suppressed.[13]

Another task is to show that despite the outcome, it was indeed a Grand Victory. Tacit US support for the slaughter of the Kurds posed some difficulties, which would have been even more severe had the media deigned to report the testimony of Western doctors and other observers on Turkish destruction of hundreds of Kurdish villages and the hundreds of thousands of Kurds in flight, trying to survive the cold winter while aid was barred by the Turkish government and Mr. Bush hailed its leader Turgut Ozal as "a protector of peace," joining those who "stand up for civilized values around the world."[14] But the tragedy of the Shi'ites, who appear to have suffered much worse destruction and terror under the gaze of the heroic Schwartzkopf, was readily put to the side; they are, after all, mere Arabs.

This task too was accomplished. In its anniversary editorial, the *Times* editors dismissed the qualms of "the doubters," concluding that the President had acted wisely. Mr. Bush had "avoided the quagmire and preserved his two triumphs: the extraordinary cooperation among coalition members and the revived self-confidence of Americans," who "greeted the Feb. 28 cease-fire with relief and pride— relief at miraculously few US casualties and pride in the brilliant performance of the allied forces," who successfully massacred an enemy that was unable to shoot back.[15] Surely these brilliant triumphs far outweigh the "awesome trage- dies" in the region.

One can appreciate the mood of the non-people of the world, rarely reported here. It is captured by Cardinal Paulo Evaristo Arns of Sao Paulo, Brazil, who writes that in the Arab countries "the rich sided with the U.S. government while the *millions* of poor condemned this military aggres- sion," while throughout the Third World "there is hatred and fear: When will they decide to invade us," and on what pretext?

Sincerely,

Noam

LOOT, 2.9, September 1991

Notes

1. *NYT*, July 28, 1991. For further detail on what follows, and sources, see my article in Peters, *Collateral Damage,* and *Deter- ring Democracy,* "Afterword."
2. *NYT*, June 24, 1991.
3. Friedman, "Week in Review," *NYT*, July 7, 1991.
4. Kathy Blair, *Toronto Globe & Mail*, June 17; Tyler, *NYT*, May 22; UN, *Guardian Weekly* (London), Aug. 4, 1991.
5. *WSJ*, July 5, 1991.

6. *Wall Street Journal,* April 8, 1991.

7. Friedman, see note 3.

8. *NYT,* Aug. 3, 1991.

9. *Mideast Mirror* (London), March 15, 1991. Cowell, *NYT,* April 11, 1991.

10. Glass, *Spectator,* London, April 13, 1991.

11. Cowell, *op. cit.* On the concept "people," see letter 4.

12. *al-Ahram,* April 9, 1991; quoted in *Mideast Mirror* (London), April 10.

13. Ron Ben-Yishai, interview with Shomron, *Ha'aretz,* March 29; Shalom Yerushalmi, "We are all with Saddam," *Kol Ha'ir,* April 4; Zak, senior editor of *Ma'ariv, Jerusalem Post,* April 4, 1991.

14. On these Turkish atrocities, barely reported here, see my article in Peters, ed. (note 1), and sources cited.

15. Editorial, *NYT,* Aug. 2, 1991.

14

The Death and Life of Stalinism

September 8, 1991

Dear *LOOT,*

The important events of late August 1991 in the Soviet Union have elicited some curious coverage and commentary. The US was a distant and passive observer, and Washington basically had no policy, simply watching events run their course. That picture, however, will not do at all.

The proper version is that the US is a benign if sometimes stern guardian of international order and morality, guiding errant elements along a constructive path. George Bush, in particular, has been assigned the image of Great Statesman, with extraordinary talent for diplomacy and global management. The picture is about as plausible as the tales of Ronald Reagan, the Great Communicator, who initiated a modern revolution—a construction quickly put to rest when this pathetic figure was no longer useful, and it could be conceded that he hadn't a thought in his head and was scarcely able to read his lines. With regard to Reagan's successor, the evidence for his consummate skills, to date, reduces to his unquestioned ability to follow the prescriptions of an early National Security Policy Review of his administration, which advised that failure to defeat "much weaker enemies...decisively and rapidly" would be "embarrassing" and might "undercut political support," understood to be thin.[1]

To reconcile reality with preferred image, there were some gestures towards Bush's allegedly critical role in bringing the August 1991 crisis to a successful conclusion. But the efforts were pretty feeble, and lacked spirit. Some, however, deserve credit for trying. Take *Boston Globe* columnist John Silber, the president of Boston University and a likely aspirant to high political office.[2] Silber parrots the standard doctrine that "the president's skill in dealing with the demise of communism heightens the disarray of the Democratic Party." In particular, "President Bush's handling of the failed coup in the USSR has been masterly. His well-publicized telephone calls to Boris Yeltsin put the United States firmly on the side of the democratic resistance, a position cemented by the shrewd decision to send Ambassador Strauss to Moscow immediately, with instructions to ignore the junta."

In the face of such brilliant and imaginative moves on the diplomatic chessboard, what can the opposition do but wring its hands in despair?

The lack of policy was evident from James Baker's briefing after the coup had collapsed. The Secretary of State presented a "four-part agenda." Three parts were the kind of pieties that speech writers produce while dozing: we want democracy, the rule of law, economic reform, settlement of security problems, etc. One part of the agenda did, however, have a modicum of substance, the item on "Soviet foreign policy." Here, Baker focused on his "efforts to convene a peace conference to launch direct negotiations and thereby to facilitate a viable peacemaking process in the Middle East." As Thomas Friedman explains in an accompanying gloss, the Soviet Union should "work together with the United States on foreign policy initiatives like Middle East peace."[3]

What is of interest here is what was missing. "Soviet foreign policy" has indeed been assigned a role in the Bush-Baker Middle East endeavor. The Soviet role is to provide a (very thin) cover for a unilateral US initiative that may at last realize the US demand, stressed by Kissinger years ago, that Europe and Japan be kept out of the diplomacy of the region. Baker's phrase "direct negotiations" is the conventional Orwellian term for the leading principle of US-Israeli rejectionism: the framework of the "peace process" must be restricted to state-to-state negotiations, effectively excluding the indigenous population and any consideration of their national rights and concerns. They offer no services to the US and, accordingly, have no meaningful rights. That is the core principle of the rigid rejectionism that the US has upheld for 20 years in virtual international isolation (apart from both major political groupings in Israel), and now feels that it may be in a position to impose.

These matters, however, fail the test of political correctness, and therefore are given no expression in the mainstream. As noted earlier in these letters, even the basic terms of the Baker-Shamir-Peres plan, to which negotiations are restricted, have fallen under this ban.

With the USSR gone from the scene, another foreign policy goal may be within reach: "replacement of the Castro regime with one more devoted to the true interests of the Cuban people and more acceptable to the U.S.," a goal that we must achieve "in such a manner as to avoid any appearance of U.S. intervention." These are the words of the March 1960 secret decision of the Eisenhower Administration that set in motion the subversion and economic warfare sharply escalated by John F. Kennedy and continued by his successors.[4]

If Washington is to achieve its longstanding goals in the required manner—avoiding "any appearance of U.S. intervention"—the ideological institutions must play their part. Crucially, they must suppress the record of aggression, vast campaigns of terror, economic strangulation, cultural quarantine, intimidation of anyone who might seek to disrupt the ban, and the other devices available to the superpower overseer dedicated to "the true interests of the Cuban people." Cuba's plight must be attributed to the demon Castro and "Cuban socialism" alone. They bear full responsibility for the "poverty, isolation and humbling dependence" on the USSR, the *New York Times* editors instruct us, concluding triumphantly that "the Cuban dictator has painted himself into his own corner," without any help from us. That being the case, by doctrinal necessity, we should not intervene directly as some "U.S. cold warriors" propose: "Fidel Castro's reign deserves to end in home-grown failure, not martyrdom." Staking their position at the dovish extreme, the editors advise that we should continue to stand aside, doing nothing, watching in silence, as we have been doing for 30 years, so the naive reader would learn from this (quite typical) version of history.[5]

The enhanced ability of the US to achieve its goals without deterrence or interference is not exactly welcome news in most of the world. But we are unlikely to hear very much about the trepidations of the Third World over "the breakdown of international military equilibrium which somehow served to contain US yearnings for domination" (Mario Benedetti). Nor were we informed of Third World reactions when Dimitri Simes, senior associate at the Carne-gie Endowment for International Peace, observed in the *New York Times* that the "apparent decline in the Soviet threat...makes military power more useful as a United States foreign policy instrument...against those who con-template challenging important American interests"—the "Soviet threat" being the deterrent to US military power and the support afforded targets of US subversion and vio-lence.[6] The fears in much of the world, however, are very real, particularly after the US-UK operations in the Gulf. They will be readily understood by anyone who can escape the doctrinal straitjacket.

The improved conditions for US subversion and vio-lence do not, however, offer the right note to sound on the occasion of the demise of the official enemy. For reflections on more exalted themes, we may turn to a think-piece by *New York Times* correspondent Richard Bernstein, who muses on the "New Issues Born From Communism's Death Knell."[7]

For more than 70 years, Bernstein explains, "the fierc-est arguments and the sharpest conflicts among intellectu-als" have been "about Marxism-Leninism and social revolution, about the nature of the Soviet Union and about the existence of Communism as a major ideological force in a bipolar world." "The most obvious power exercised by the Soviet Union over the Western mind," he continues, "was its extraordinary power of attraction, its capacity to instill idealistic visions of a new world in which exploitation would be swept away by a tide of revolution." After the appeal of the USSR itself faded, "the debate took on new forms": "[F]rom the 1960's to the 1980's, an argument raged...about...countries like China, Ethiopia, Cuba and Nicaragua, which seemed to many on the left to embody the revolutionary virtues admittedly tarnished in the Soviet Union itself." Throughout, the Cold War conflict "had the effect of polarizing the domestic debate" in the US between these two ideological extremes, Harvard Professor Joseph Nye observes. But with "the debate about Communism" losing "its force and centrality," Bernstein asks, "what issues will consume left and right, liberals and conservatives, in the future?" Perhaps the newspapers and journals of opinion will expire, now that the all-consuming issues are dying away, so that debate over them is no longer "raging" in their pages.

Let us put aside the accuracy of this account of "the left"; and, for the sake of argument, let us also accept the picture of "the arguments and conflicts" that have "polarized the domestic debate" for over 70 years. We now ask a simple question. How has this central debate of the modern era been reflected in the *New York Times*, the Newspaper of Record, dedicated to the highest standards of journalistic integrity, free and open to all shades of thought and opinion?

The question has, in fact, been investigated, beginning with the classic 1920 study of *Times* coverage of the Bolshevik revolution by Walter Lippmann and Charles Merz, who demonstrated that it was "nothing short of a disaster...from the point of view of professional journalism," merely vulgar jingoism and subservience to the state both in editorial policy and in the news columns that this policy "profoundly and crassly influenced." Moving to the present, there has been extensive study of *Times* coverage of the most controversial issue of the 1980s, the "raging" issue of Nicaragua; it demonstrates that the Lippmann-Merz critique remains quite accurate. News coverage was, as usual, "profoundly and crassly influenced" by the doctrine of service to state power that defines the editorial stance. Even columns and Op-Eds were restricted, with startling uniformity, to the politically correct doctrine that the Sandinista curse must be expunged and Nicaragua restored to the "regional standards" of such more acceptable models as El Salvador and Guatemala. In the years between, the record is much the same as in these two extraordinary cases.[8]

It is true that not every topic has been investigated. Thus, I do not know of studies of *Times* coverage of the "raging debate" over the revolutionary virtues of Ethiopia's Mengistu or of the welcome the *Times* has offered to articles illustrating the "extraordinary power of attraction" of Marxism-Leninism and its "capacity to instill idealistic visions" of revolution and utopia. Even if we translate these rhetorical flights to something resembling reality, however, we know exactly what we will discover about just how open the Newspaper of Record has been to debate, discussion, even inconvenient fact.

The tale now concocted—perhaps even believed—is of some interest. For more than 70 years the *New York Times* (hardly alone, of course) and state-corporate power have marched in impressive unison. Now, hearing "Communism's Death Knell," it is permissible to concede that there were some issues that might have been allowed an occasional word of discussion, though not to present them in a sane and meaningful form, even in retrospect. Meanwhile the record of lock-step conformism is transmuted to a raging debate so remote from reality as scarcely to reach the level of the comical. It is, evidently, a matter of some importance to suppress even a faint flicker of recognition that the real issues have been virtually excluded from the doctrinal system. An intriguing performance.

The "death knell" of Soviet tyranny has indeed sounded, though what takes its place may also not be too pleasant to behold. But Stalinist values remain alive and well, and the cultural commissars have no end of work ahead of them.

Sincerely,

Noam

Notes

1. Maureen Dowd, *NYT*, Feb. 23, 1991.
2. "Democrats' disarray boosts Bush's apparent invulnerability," *BG*, Sept 1, 1991.
3. "Baker's Remarks: Policy on Soviets," *NYT*; Friedman, *NYT*, A1, Sept. 5, 1991.
4. Jules R. Benjamin, *The United States and the Origins of the Cuban Revolution* (Princeton, 1990), 207.
5. Editorial, *NYT*, Sept. 8, 1991.
6. Benedetti, *La Epoca*, Chile, May 4, 1991, echoing the reactions expressed by Cardinal Evaristo Arns, cited in letter 13, and many others throughout the Third World. Simes, "If the Cold War Is Over, Then What?," *NYT*, Dec. 27, 1988.
7. *NYT*, Aug. 31, 1991, A1.
8. See *Necessary Illusions* for extensive discussion; also, *Manufacturing Consent*, among many other sources.

15

Toxic Omissions

October 7, 1991

Dear *LOOT*,

We can learn a good deal about the way the world works by observing what fails to reach the threshold in the ideological institutions, remaining invisible. Academic studies are sometimes instructive in this regard. In the *Political Science Quarterly*, Doris Graber reviews Nicholas Berry's *Foreign Policy and the Press: An Analysis of The New York Times' Coverage of U.S. Foreign Policy*, "a must-read for anyone interested in how the press covers foreign policy." Berry's study "confirmed his theory and disconfirmed its rivals." His theory is that "If policies turn out to be failures, the media feature the views of vocal critics," though only "credible, quotable, political sources" need apply. The disconfirmed rival theories are not identified, but they must be theories that claim that the servility of the media reaches such extraordinary heights that they refuse even to criticize failure. All advocates of the view that the US media surpass totalitarianism are therefore properly chastized.[1]

Unworthy of even disconfirming are theories that entertain the subversive thought that it might not be enough for the media to be obedient servants, adopting the doctrines of the powerful without critical analysis and evaluating them only in terms acceptable within the corridors of power: success or failure. Those with such expectations for a free society are too far out even to be perceived in the intellectual culture.

Omissions in major stories of the past month reveal interesting tacit assumptions that guide policy and shape its doctrinal disguises. One focus of attention was the confirmation hearings for Robert Gates as CIA director. As they ended, Elaine Sciolino reviewed the record, identifying the Big Questions: the candidate's contrition and arrogance, his "character and style," the sincerity of "his personal confession," etc.[2] One sentence in her summary notes that Gates "believed that direct military action was the only way to deal with the Sandinista government in Nicaragua," but Sciolino rightly ignores this marginal issue, which did not interest Congress or the press.

The reference is to a memorandum of December 14, 1984 from Gates to CIA chief William Casey.[3] The deputy director for intelligence opens by stating that "It is time to talk absolutely straight about Nicaragua." We must "accept that ridding the Continent of this regime is important to our national interest." We must dispense with the "fig leaf of curtailing the flow of arms to El Salvador" and other pretenses that "can easily be politically dismissed" (though they continued to be trotted out by the *Times* and other loyalists when needed). We must pursue "a comprehensive campaign openly aimed at bringing down this regime," adopting whatever means are necessary, including economic sanctions (soon instituted) and, if feasible, "quarantine" and military force (air strikes, etc.). "Hopes of causing the regime to reform itself for a more pluralistic government are essentially silly and hopeless," Gates wrote immediately after the 1984 elections, which were illegitimate because victory of US clients ("pluralism") could not be enforced. Either we recognize "that the Western Hemisphere is the sphere of influence of the United States," so that we may "rid the Continent" of anyone we do not like by whatever means we choose, or we decide "totally to abandon the Monroe Doctrine."

These thoughts do not bear on Gates's qualifications. Also unnoticed is the fact that he has solid grounds for his interpretation of the Monroe Doctrine, for example, the observations by Woodrow Wilson's Secretary of State Robert Lansing:

In its advocacy of the Monroe Doctrine the United States considers its own interests. The integrity of other American nations is an incident, not an end. While this may seem based on selfishness alone, the author of the Doctrine had no higher or more generous motive in its declaration.

President Wilson found Lansing's argument "unanswerable," though he felt it "impolitic" to make it public. Evidently, little has changed in 75 years.

An indirect affirmation of the same stance appears in Vincent Canby's favorable review of a film by Susan Meiselas, which, he notes, reflects her pro-Sandinista sympathies.[4] The film, Canby relates, is "a somber meditation on what sometimes looks like the futility of all social struggle." Apart from a few vague phrases about "outside pressures," the reader is left in the dark about certain rather important reasons for the "futility"—accurately revealed in the Gates memorandum and the reaction to it.

Basic assumptions are revealed further in the lack of response to Bush's opposition to economic sanctions against the coup regime of Haiti: "the problem with that one is you start hurting the Haitian people."[5] Silence is appropriate; it would be superfluous to point out the utter hypocrisy of the comment in the light of Bush's record. The tacit assumption is that the President is, of course, a thuggish hypocrite whose declarations are not taken seriously by any sane person, and are merely a cover for our shared intent to rule the hemisphere—indeed the world—by any means necessary, ridding our domains of anyone who gets in our way.

Omissions in the September 26 issue of the *Times* obliquely illustrate the same assumptions. In a front-page story on Iraq, Andrew Rosenthal quotes without comment a US official: "If you're going to build any kind of credibility for a new world order, you've got to make people accountable to legal procedures, and Saddam's flaunted every one."[6] On the back pages, the same day, we find an excerpt from a Reuters dispatch headed "U.S. Forgives $260 Million

Managua Debt." Excised from the dispatch is a paragraph reporting that a few days earlier Nicaragua had dropped the World Court suit against the US.[7] That action had not merited report in the *Times*, and was barely noted elsewhere.[8] A year earlier, the *Times* had casually observed that US aid was being withheld to coerce Nicaragua to abandon "the judgment of as much as $17 billion that Nicaragua won against the United States at the International Court of Justice."[9] The silences of September 26 provide a perfect backdrop for our stern injunction that all must be "accountable to legal procedures" if our "new world order" is to be credible.

Other stories of the month go on routinely about the President's "great dreams" and "vision on the future," the "historic window of opportunity" afforded by the triumph of US arms and the collapse of the Evil Empire, etc., etc. Two factors have made it possible for Bush "to dream such great dreams" about Israel-Arab peace and other matters, R.W. Apple observes: (1) there is now no fear that "regional tensions" might lead to superpower confrontation; (2) "no longer must the United States contend with countries whose cantankerousness was reinforced by Moscow's interest in continuing unrest."[10]

The factors are accurately identified, but a translation from Newspeak is needed. Factor (1) is that with the Soviet deterrent gone, the US can now use force freely to impose its will, a consequence that, not surprisingly, evokes fear and desperation throughout much of the world. Point (2) expresses the conventional doctrine that the US stand is necessarily right and just, so that those who oppose it are "cantankerous" agents of Soviet disruption. In the case under discussion, this category includes all NATO allies, the non-aligned countries, indeed virtually every state in the world except Israel and the US, as illustrated by the annual UN votes calling for opening the peace process that the US has always barred because it conflicts with US rejectionism. But the historical facts, reviewed earlier, have been expunged with such efficiency that the commissars need not fear that some Winston Smith will plaintively recall that $2+2 = 4$.

Similar achievements underlie the nod of approval for PLO "realism" in authorizing Palestinians who are granted US-Israeli approval to attend the US-run "peace conference," where they will be permitted to "negotiate" their acceptance of the Shamir plan but to discuss nothing else, as James Baker explained unambiguously in late 1989. An editorial in the *Boston Globe* is typical.[11] It states that "the principal causes of the PLO's weakness are the defeat of Saddam Hussein, the political and monetary cost of Arafat's alliance with Saddam, and the evanescence of the Soviet superpower." PLO crimes, the editors relate, include the failure to expel the perpetrators of a thwarted terrorist action in May 1990, which led to the cancellation of the US-PLO dialogue, and Arafat's support for Iraq's conquest of Kuwait (which the PLO publicly opposed).

These doctrines are convenient for advocates of US-Israeli rejectionism. Their falsity is readily demonstrated by the fact that the Bush-Baker conditions were imposed while the US-PLO "dialogue" was proceeding in 1989, long before the invasion of Kuwait, and without the slightest concern for the Soviet Union. Furthermore, the Bush-Baker plan simply perpetuated the US rejection of Palestinian rights, in opposition to virtually the entire world. As for the US-PLO dialogue, it opened with the demand by the US that the PLO abandon any hope for a nonrejectionist international conference and call off the "riots" (the Intifada), "which we view as terrorist acts against Israel," thus restoring the status quo. Israel's Defense Minister, Yitzhak Rabin of the Labor Party, welcomed the sham dialogue as a device to grant Israel time to crush the Intifada by force, as it proceeded to do. The facts having been barred by the guardians of political correctness, the editors and their colleagues are free to invent history to suit doctrinal needs.

If inconvenient truths were not beyond the pale, some curious journalist might ask about the origins of the Israeli law that bars contacts with those designated "terrorists," and is used to deny Palestinians the right to select their own representatives for negotiations, and to jail Israeli peace activists and other undesirables who meet PLO representatives. A leading Israeli legal commentator, Moshe Negbi, provides the answer in an article headlined "The Law to Prevent Contact with the Head of State." Negbi reports that the law barring contact with terrorists was instituted at "the personal initiative of head of state [David] Ben-Gurion"; its specific targets were Yitzhak Shamir and his fellow-terrorists, who had just murdered UN mediator Folke Bernadotte, a considerable embarrassment for the new State of Israel in late 1948. These proscriptions were not officially revoked until the Likud victory of 1977.[12] A serious journal might also contemplate the more general consequences of the condition that advocates of terror are to be barred from the negotiating table. We'll wait a long time for that.

Another major story of the past month was Bush's initiative to reduce nuclear weapons. Again, some background was missing. Standard doctrine, across the spectrum, is that nuclear weapons have been needed as a "shield" for intervention, so that the US could pursue its "global interests" by "conventional means or theater forces," which can serve as "meaningful instruments of military and political power" under the "nuclear umbrella" (Reaganite Eugene Rostow, Carter Defense Secretary Harold Brown). With the "umbrella" no longer needed, it can be (partially) folded, though the instruments of coercion must remain at the ready for use against the traditional victims. The basic point was explained by the respected statesman Lloyd George after British pressure had prevented the 1932 disarmament convention from banning bombardment of civilians: "We insisted on reserving the right to bomb niggers," he observed forthrightly. That remains the bottom line, whether the "umbrella" is needed or not.[13]

Those who regard themselves as "on the left" might be

heartened by another omission, this one in a front-page *Times* story by Anthony DePalma on the "new leftist orthodoxy mockingly called political correctness."[14] DePalma reviews the condemnation of this "orthodoxy" by President Bush and many others, who claim that opponents of racism, sexism, etc., are posing a dangerous threat to the freedom that has hitherto reigned on campus. Suppose, for the sake of argument, we grant the accuracy of all the condemnations and the implicit claims about the golden age before the new orthodoxy established its iron grip. Still, one obvious question comes to mind. Why is it taken for granted, across the board, that to oppose racism and sexism, and to call for respect for other cultures, is a "leftist" position—hence by implication, one that decent folk must abjure? The tacit assumption is not addressed. Its implications are not without interest.

Sincerely,

Noam

LOOT, 2.11, November 1991

Notes

1. Graber, *PSQ*, Summer 1991.
2. "Hearings on Gates Show Many Layers of His Personality," *NYT*, Oct. 6, 1991, 1.
3. *NYT*, Sept. 20, 1991.
4. *NYT*, Oct. 5, 1991.
5. Thomas Friedman, "U.S. and Latins Moving to Isolate Haiti," *NYT*, Oct. 3, 1991, last paragraph.
6. "The Bush-Hussein Duel," *NYT*, Sept. 26.
7. Reuters, *Boston Globe*, "US writes off Nicaragua's debt," Sept. 26, 1991, p. 13.
8. *BG*, "Nicaragua drops suit against US," Sept. 18, 1991, p. 70.
9. Mark Uhlig, "U.S. Urges Nicaragua to Forgive Legal Claim," *NYT*, Sept. 30, 1990. In 1992, the US withheld over $100 million of aid from Nicaragua, the pretext this time being a series of wild charges emanating from Senator Jesse Helms's office (half was later released). The noose is likely to be kept

tight, or at least dangling, until the government lives up to US standards of subordination; see letter 10.

10. Apple, "Is Time Running Out for Bush to Remake the Middle East?," *NYT* "Week in Review," Sept. 22, 1991, p. 1.

11. Editorial, *BG,* Oct. 6.

12. Negbi, *Hadashot,* Sept. 13, 1991. On current use of the law against Jews, see Clyde Haberman, "Israel Jails Abie Nathan for New Arafat Contact," *NYT,* Oct. 7, 1991.

13. Rostow, Brown, cited in *On Power and Ideology,* 105. Lloyd George, cited by V.G. Kiernan, *European Empires from Conquest to Collapse* (Fontana, 1982), 200.

14. "In Campus Debate On New Orthodoxy, A Counteroffensive," *NYT,* Sept. 25, 1991.

16
"Fiendish Acts"

December 8, 1991

Dear *LOOT*,

The lead headlines on November 15 blared out "U.S. ACCUSES LIBYA AS 2 ARE CHARGED IN PAN AM BOMBING," "RETALIATION HINTED" for an "attack that killed 270 people and became a horrific symbol of terrorism." It was a "fiendish act of wickedness [which] cannot be passed over or ignored," British Foreign Secretary Douglas Hurd declaimed. Investigators in "The worldwide detective case" ranged over 50 countries, questioning 14,000 people, and "examined hundreds of thousands of bits of debris combed from an 845-square-mile area." Editorials issued stern calls for punishment. The indictment "raises profound questions," the *Times* editors observed, posing "a challenge to nations to complete the task of doing international justice...aggressively, but judiciously." *Washington Post* editors hailed the "prodigious investigation," calling on the US "to deal otherwise with his regime" if Qaddafi does not extradite the suspects, recalling the bombing of Tripoli in 1986, when the US murdered dozens of civilians because it "felt sure" that Libya was responsible for a disco bombing in West Berlin—with no credible evidence, as the German investigators informed American reporters who kept the facts under wraps, and as the media later quietly conceded.[1]

The reaction was not entirely uniform. The *Times* ran an Op-Ed by leading terrorologists pointing out that the evidence concerning Libya was thin and the indictment a matter of "political expedience," avoiding "the real masterminds" (Iran and Syria) and "let[ting] the Palestinians off the hook." The authors are Robert and Tamara Kupperman, the former a leading proponent of Low Intensity Conflict

117

(LIC) and the author of manuals on how to conduct it efficiently. LIC, as Kupperman defines it, is the threat or use of
force "to achieve political objectives without the full-scale
commitment of resources." LIC is to be distinguished from
"terrorism," defined in a US Army Manual as the threat or
use of violence "to attain goals that are political, religious,
or ideological in nature." The subtle commissar will readily
perceive the distinction between LIC (noble, *our* policy) and
terrorism (fiendish, *their* policy).[2]

The government of Israel too was "convinced that
Palestinian terrorists based in Syria" were responsible,"
Clyde Haberman reported from Jerusalem. The following
day, columnist A.M. Rosenthal denounced President Bush
for avoiding "the proven Syrian-Palestinian involvement."
Two weeks before, Rosenthal had been presented with the
Defender of Jerusalem Award at a ceremony in New York
for his "extraordinary devotion to the protection of Jewish
rights" as "a proud Jew, unafraid to speak his mind," serv-
ing "as a calm, reasoned and yet passionate voice on Jewish
and Israeli affairs."[3]

In short, there was a spectrum of responses. At one
extreme, we have those who take the government case to be
proven on the grounds that it was proclaimed. At the other
are the skeptics, leading proponents of international terrorism and Defenders of Jerusalem, who adopt Israel's position that its enemies have been "let off the hook" and
should be relentlessly pursued, taking its case to be proven
on the grounds that it was proclaimed. The technical term
for this display is "an Independent Press in a Free Society."

A number of topics were not discussed, just as they
have not been discussed before. One case that comes to
mind is the worst air tragedy of the decade, the blowing up
of an Air India flight in 1985 off the coast of Ireland, with
329 people killed. The bombers were traced to a paramilit-
ary camp in Alabama where mercenaries were trained for
terrorist acts (LIC) in Central America and elsewhere. According to ex-mercenaries, the camp director had close ties

to U.S. intelligence and was personally involved in the Air India bombing, allegedly a "sting" operation that got out of control. On a visit to India a few months later, Attorney-General Edwin Meese conceded in a backhanded way that the terrorist operations originated in a US terrorist training camp. Lacking an inquiry questioning 14,000 people and extending over an 845-square-mile area, we know little more about this operation—though it is likely that inquiries in one or two countries, not 50, would shed some light on the matter. We do know one thing, however: it was not "a horrific symbol of terrorism" or a "fiendish act of wickedness" that must be punished.[4]

There was another air tragedy, also killing more innocents than the bombing of Pan Am 103, that could not be entirely ignored: "the accidental downing of an Iranian passenger jet over the Persian Gulf by the USS Vincennes in 1988," killing 290 people, which may have provoked the Lockerbie bombing (Mary Curtius).[5] The *Vincennes* was part of a naval armada dispatched to the Gulf to assist Bush's friend Saddam Hussein, then facing problems in his war of aggression against Iran. Shortly before the *Vincennes* shot down the Iranian airbus, its helicopters sank two Iranian speedboats. "In the wake of the Iranian airbus disaster," the culmination of Washington's "diplomatic, military and economic campaign" in support of Saddam Hussein, Iran faced reality and effectively capitulated to "Baghdad and Washington," which had "co-ordinate[d] their military operations against Teheran" (Dilip Hiro).[6]

We might ask how the news columns can be so sure that the downing of the Iranian passenger jet was "accidental," apart from doctrinal necessity. Not everyone agrees. There is, for example, US Navy Commander David Carlson, who "wondered aloud in disbelief" as he observed from his nearby vessel as the *Vincennes*—then within Iranian territorial waters—shot down what was obviously a civilian airliner in a commercial corridor, perhaps out of "a need to prove the viability of Aegis," its high tech missile system.[7]

The Commander of the *Vincennes* did not go unpunished. In April 1990, George Bush conferred upon him the Legion of Merit award (along with the officer in charge of anti-air warfare) for "exceptionally meritorious conduct in the performance of outstanding service" and for the "calm and professional atmosphere" under his command during the period when the airliner was shot down. "The tragedy isn't mentioned in the texts of the citations," AP reported. The media kept a dutiful silence—at home, that is. In the less disciplined Third World, the facts were reported in reviews of US terrorism.[8]

Iran called on the World Court to order reparations for the crime. In March 1991, Washington once again—as in the case of its terrorist war against Nicaragua—rejected World Court jurisdiction.[9] Commentators here were too mesmerized by our noble defense of international law in the Gulf to notice.

In Britain, Paul Wilkinson, the director of a leading academic Research Institute for the Study of Terrorism, responded sharply to a challenge to the US right to demand that Libya hand over the Lockerbie bombers in the light of the Iranian airbus tragedy and US atrocities generally. The "arguments are specious," he declared loftily. In the former case, the US government "admitted to the tragic error" and "at least offered some compensation to the victims' families"; and the fact that "the US has been a belligerent in a number of wars in which many have been killed...does not justify attacks on innocent civilians."[10] Wilkinson's first response omits a few pertinent facts, as just noted. His second response is surely correct, but intriguing. Trivially, the fact that country X is a "belligerent in a war in which many were killed" does not justify atrocities by some unrelated country Y; one wonders why the point was made. More interesting is the phrasing, which is accurate to the degree that it would be accurate to describe the USSR as a "belligerent in a war in which many were killed" in Afghanistan, or Hitler in Poland, or Japan in Manchuria.

There are no surprises here. Like Walter Laqueur and other respectable scholars, Wilkinson adheres to the convention that terrorism and aggression count as such when attributable to official enemies, while crimes conducted by the states one serves are exempt from such categories.[11] The same is true of their counterparts in totalitarian states, who at least can plead fear in extenuation.

Foreign Minister Hurd follows the same conventions. Needless to say, atrocities carried out by the UK or the boss in Washington do not count as "fiendish acts of wickedness." The same is true of favored friends such as Saddam Hussein or General Suharto. Thus in February 1990, when the White House was rebuffing Iraqi democrats calling for parliamentary democracy in Iraq, the British Foreign Office cooperated by impeding their efforts to condemn Iraqi terror publicly, for fear that it might harm Anglo-Iraqi relations. Two months later, after the execution of London *Observer* correspondent Farzad Bazoft and other atrocities, Hurd reiterated the need to maintain relations with Iraq.[12]

A few months later, when Saddam committed his sole crime (disobeying orders), we were treated to much uplifting rhetoric about the sanctity of international law and the newly-discovered principle that aggressors must be brutally punished without negotiation. Meanwhile, Indonesia used the occasion to launch another major military operation in the annexed territory of East Timor, where its near-genocidal campaign far surpassed the horrors of Iraq's invasion of Kuwait. Britain again offered its cooperation. British Aerospace entered into new arrangements to sell Indonesia jet fighters along with co-production arrangements, "what could turn out to be one of the largest arms packages any company has sold to an Asean country," the *Far Eastern Economic Review* reported, while atrocities mounted and Australia firmed up its new agreement with Indonesia to rob Timorese oil.[13] Western civilization is not short of uplifting acts, and eloquent spokespersons to expound our high ideals.

On November 18, at the height of the furor over Libya's refusal to hand over the suspected killers, the Foreign Minister of Costa Rica urged once again that the US comply with international extradition treaties and hand over John Hull, charged with premeditated homicide, trafficking in arms and drugs, and other criminal acts, in particular, participation in the 1984 bombing of a news conference at La Penca in which six people were killed.[14] Costa Rica had formally requested the extradition in April. To my knowledge, neither the renewed Costa Rican request nor US response (if any) was reported.

It is not that terrorism in Costa Rica never reaches threshold. The preceding February, Washington froze $10 million of promised economic aid in reaction to terrorist atrocities far surpassing the La Penca or Lockerbie bombings. The case involved land owned by US businessman Joseph Hamilton that Costa Rica, under severe pressures from Washington, had allowed to be used for a secret airstrip to violate a congressional ban on US arms for the contras. When the facts were revealed, Costa Rican President Arias ordered the land confiscated and turned over to the Santa Rosa National Park. But Hamilton (with other businessmen) claims that he was not adequately compensated, and the US Government, always a stern defender of human rights, withheld the aid in retaliation.[15]

The brazen arrogance of the powerful passes far beyond the imagination of ordinary mortals.

With the backing of the Arab League, Libya offered to submit the US-UK charges to "neutral international committees of inquiry or to the International Court of Justice." Professor Alfred Rubin of the Fletcher School of Law and Diplomacy made the simple point that "if the charge [against Libya] is serious, there is everything to gain and nothing to lose by presenting the case to the International Court of Justice as Libya proposes."[16] The Bush Administration flatly rejected any neutral inquiry, AP reported. Rubin's logic is impeccable. Few will pursue it.

The most insightful media comment I saw on the whole affair was by the person responsible for the layout of the front page of the *Boston Globe*. Adjacent to the lead story on the charge against Libya, there is a report opening "President Bush plans to counter public concern over his domestic policies."[17] That seems to sum it up nicely.

In fact, Libya has been used as a punching bag for domestic purposes since mid-1981.[18] As the effects of the Reagan-Bush assault against the population become more difficult to conceal, we may look forward to replays of the scenario of the past years: awesome enemy, miraculous triumph by heroic leader. It is not easy to find methods to prevent the public from attending to the welfare state for the rich constructed by the statist reactionaries of the past decade, even beyond the norm, the costs to be paid by the majority of the population and future generations.

Sincerely,

Noam

Notes

1. Andrew Rosenthal, *NYT*, A1; David Johnston, *NYT*, A8; Nov. 15, 1991. Editorials, *NYT*, Nov. 16; *WP weekly*, Nov. 25, 1991. On what was known, and what was concealed, at the time of the Libya bombing, see *Pirates & Emperors*, chap. 3.
2. *NYT*, Nov. 16, 1991. See *Necessary Illusions* (*NI*), 270.
3. Haberman, *NYT*, Nov. 21. Rosenthal, *NYT*, Nov. 22; award, *Jerusalem Post*, Nov. 7, 1991.
4. *NI*, 271.
5. "2 Libyans charged in Pan Am blast," *Boston Globe*, Nov. 15, 1991.
6. Hiro, *The Longest War* (Routledge 1991), 211f., 239f.
7. Carlson, *U.S. Naval Institute Proceedings*, Sept. 1989; Carlson, *Los Angeles Times* Op-Ed, Sept. 3, 1989.
8. AP, April 23, 1990; *Third World Resurgence*, Malaysia, Oct. 1990. In 1992, *Newsweek*, which had previously parroted the government line, broke ranks and reported the long-known

facts: John Barry and Roger Charles, "Sea of Lies," *Newsweek* July 13, 1992. See Jim Sibbison, *LOOT,* Sept. 1992, for a review of *Newsweek's* 1988 and 1992 versions.

9. *Chicago Tribune,* March 6, 1991.

10. *Manchester Guardian Weekly,* Dec. 8, 1991.

11. On Wilkinson's record, see Alexander George, in George, ed., *Western State Terrorism*. On Laqueur, see my essay in the same volume, and *NI,* 277-82. On the "scholarly" record more generally, see Herman and O'Sullivan, *'Terrorism' Industry*.

12. See my essay in Peters, ed., *Collateral Damage*.

13. *FEER,* July 25, 1991. See *Year 501,* chap. 5, and sources cited, for further detail and background.

14. AP, Nov. 19, 1991.

15. *Central America Report,* Guatemala, Feb. 15, 1991.

16. AP, *BG,* Nov. 16; Tony Walker, *Financial Times* (London), Dec. 6; Rubin, "The US and Britain Should Take Libya to Court," *Christian Science Monitor,* Dec. 2, 1991.

17. John Mashek, "Bush domestic plan reported in the works; Aides cite concern on standing in polls," *BG,* Nov. 15, 1991.

18. For a review, see *Pirates & Emperors,* chap. 3.

17
The PC Thought Police

April 6, 1992

Dear *LOOT*,

Media critique has generally focused on how the news and opinion sections ensure right thinking. Book reviews are another intriguing element of the system of doctrinal control. In particular, the *New York Times Book Review* serves as a guide to readers and librarians with limited resources. The editors must not only select the right books, but also reviewers who adhere to the norms of political correctness. What follows are some illustrations, drawn from three successive weeks last month (March 1992).

In the study of any system, it is often useful to consider something radically different, to highlight crucial features. Let's begin, then, by looking at a society that is close to the opposite pole from ours: Brezhnev's USSR.

Consider policy formation. In Brezhnev's USSR, economic policy was determined in secret, by centralized power; popular involvement was nil, except marginally, through the Communist Party. Political decisions were pretty much in the same hands. The political system was meaningless, with virtually no flow from bottom to top.

Consider next the information system, inevitably constrained by the distribution of economic-political power. In Brezhnev's USSR there was a spectrum, bounded by disagreements within centralized power. True, the media were never obedient enough for the commissars. Thus they were bitterly condemned for undermining public morale during the war in Afghanistan, playing into the hands of the imperial aggressors and their local agents from whom the USSR was courageously defending the people of Afghanistan.[1] For the totalitarian mind, no degree of servility is ever enough.

There were dissidents and alternative media: under-ground *samizdat* and foreign radio. According to a 1979 US government-funded study, 77 percent of blue-collar work-ers and 96 percent of the middle elite listened to foreign broadcasts, while the alternative press reached 45 percent of high-level professionals, 41 percent of political leaders, 27 percent of managers, and 14 percent of blue-collar workers. The study also found most people satisfied with living con-ditions, favoring state-provided medical care, and largely supportive of state control of heavy industry. Emigration was more for personal than political reasons: "economic refugees," to use accurately the term regularly applied to exclude from our shores unworthy victims who flee terror by US-supported gangsters.[2]

Dissidents were bitterly condemned as "anti-Soviet" and "supporters of capitalist imperialism," as demon-strated by the fact that they condemned the evils of the Soviet system and its policies instead of marching in pa-rades denouncing the crimes of official enemies. They were also punished, not in the style of US dependencies such as El Salvador, but harshly enough.

The concept "anti-Soviet" is particularly striking. We find similar concepts in Nazi Germany, Brazil under the neo-Nazi Generals, and totalitarian cultures generally. In a relatively free society, the concept would simply evoke rid-icule. Imagine, say, the reaction in Milan or Florence if some Italian critic of state power were condemned for "anti-Italianism." Such concepts as "anti-Soviet" are the very hallmark of a totalitarian culture; only the most dedicated and humorless commissar could use such terms with a straight face.

Well-behaved party hacks were guilty of no such crimes as anti-Sovietism. Their task was to applaud the state and its leaders; or even better, to criticize them for occa-sional deviation from their grand principles, thus instilling the propaganda line by presupposition rather than assertion, always the most effective technique. The commissar might say that leaders erred in their defense of Afghanistan against "the assault from the inside, which was manipulated" by Pakistan and the CIA. They should have understood that "it was an Afghan war, and if we converted it into a white man's war, we would lose." Similarly, a Nazi ideologue might have conceded that the "encounter" between Germans and Slavs on the Eastern front was "less than inspiring," though for balance, we must recall that it was "a total war between rival nations for control of a territory both groups were willing to die for"; and for the Slavs "the terms of the conflict" were "less mortal" than for the Germans needing *Lebensraum*, "staking not only their fortunes but also their very lives on the hope of building new lives in untried country." The Slavs, after all, could trudge off to Siberia. I return to the source of the quotes directly.

With these observations as background, let us turn to our own free society.

Let's begin again with policy formation. Economic policy is determined in secret; in law and in principle, popular involvement is nil. The Fortune 500 are more diverse than the Politburo, and market mechanisms provide far more diversity than in a command economy. But a corporation, factory, or business is the economic equivalent of fascism: decisions and control are strictly top-down. People are not compelled to purchase the products or rent themselves to survive, but those are the sole choices for most of the population.

The political system is closely linked to economic power, both through personnel and broader constraints on policy. Efforts of the public to enter the political arena must be barred: liberal elites see such efforts as a dangerous "crisis of democracy," and they are intolerable to statist reactionaries ("conservatives," in contemporary Newspeak). The political system has virtually no flow from bottom to top, apart from the local level; the general public appears to regard it as largely meaningless.

The media present a spectrum of opinion, largely re-
flecting tactical divisions within the state-corporate nexus.
True, they are never obedient enough for the commissars.
The media were bitterly condemned for undermining public
morale during the war in Vietnam, playing into the hands of
the imperial aggressors and their local agents from whom
the US was courageously defending the people of Vietnam;
a Freedom House study provides a dramatic example.[3] For
the totalitarian mind, again, no degree of servility is enough.

There are dissidents and other information sources.
Foreign radio broadcasts reach virtually no one, but alternative media exist, though without a tiny fraction of the out-
reach of *samizdat*. Dissidents are bitterly condemned as
"anti-American" and "supporters of Communism" as demonstrated by the fact that they condemn the evils of the
American system and its policies instead of marching in
parades denouncing the crimes of official enemies. But they
are not severely punished, at least if they are privileged and
of the right color. "Responsible intellectuals" are guilty of
no such crime as "anti-Americanism." Rather, they perform
their task, applauding the state and its leaders, or even
better, criticizing them for occasional deviation from their
grand principles, thus instilling the propaganda line by presupposition rather than assertion.

Once again, the concept "anti-American" is particularly striking, the very hallmark of a totalitarian mentality.

Let us now turn to the *Times Book Review*, keeping to
the reviews, not the books.

The March 15 issue carries Morton Kondracke's review of Paul Hollander's book *Anti-Americanism*. Both the
author and the reviewer are loyal apologists for atrocities by
the US government and its clients. Kondracke applauds this
worthy exposure of the crime of anti-Americanism, though
he feels Hollander may go too far when he cites benefits for
the handicapped as an illustration of the leftist deviation of
Congress.

"Anti-Americanism" (equivalently "the left," or "Marxists") is defined by the author as "a generally critical disposition toward existing social arrangements," the "cultural belief" that "this is a severely flawed and possibly doomed society, though still a menace to its citizens and humanity." Kondracke agrees that "the left gets more respect and attention in the news media than its ideas merit," and is "strongly influential" in colleges and the church. But all is not lost: "there is not a single Marxist or 'anti-American' major daily newspaper (or even major newspaper columnist) in the country" and the "mainline churches" (dangerous anti-Americans) are losing membership. Fortunately, those with "a generally critical disposition toward existing social arrangements" are almost entirely silenced, though we must keep up our guard in case the heresy finds a tiny outlet.

Kondracke is particularly outraged that even though "the Communist alternative has collapsed," the anti-Americans (by implication, pro-Communists) maintain their "permanently adversarial culture" and continue to "hate their nation." They "have not recanted," even though they have been proven "disastrously wrong" in their wild claims that the Sandinistas and other evil-doers "represented a bright future for mankind"—or, to replace raving by reality, that the Sandinistas might have offered hope for Nicaraguans. The criminals in this case include the World Bank, Central American Jesuits, the leading figure of Central American democracy, José Figueres, a great enthusiast for US corporations and the CIA, indeed, a rather broad range. But that just shows how awesome the anti-American conspiracy is. Fortunately, readers of the *Times* were carefully protected from any awareness of the scale of such "anti-Americanism," and in this and numerous other ways saved from possible infection by the plague.[4]

Kondracke does not remind us how the anti-Americans were refuted, though his record suggests that he would agree with *Time* magazine's admiring review of the technique that brought about the latest of the "happy series of democratic surprises" as "democracy burst forth" in Nicaragua in February 1990: to "wreck the economy and prosecute a long and deadly proxy war until the exhausted natives overthrow the unwanted government themselves," with a cost to us that is "minimal," leaving the victim "with wrecked bridges, sabotaged power stations, and ruined farms," and thus providing the US candidate with "a winning issue": ending the "impoverishment of the people of Nicaragua." Kondracke's enthusiasm for terrorist violence and illegal economic warfare with its happy consequences (starvation, disease, infant deaths, etc.) was no less avid; and his love of "democracy" is of the same order.[5]

The anti-Americans, Kondracke explains, are driven only by "the pleasure of struggle against the world in which they live." Evidence is unnecessary. How else could one possibly explain their "generally critical disposition toward existing social arrangements"? But, he concludes triumphantly, "for all their raving against America, few America-haters ever leave." Love it or leave it, but don't dare to say that its magnificence is flawed. Totalitarian cultures do not often reach such heights.

In the next week's issue (March 22), Caleb Carr reviews a book on the 1862 Sioux Uprising in Minnesota. After the obligatory frothing at the mouth about the evils of PC left-fascism, Carr explains that the "Minnesota encounter" was "a total war between rival nations for control of a territory both groups were willing to die for." For one nation, "settlement was generally their last hope"; they were "staking not only their fortunes but also their very lives on the hope of building new lives in untried country." For the natives, at least at first, "the terms of the conflict" were "less mortal"; they could, after all, trudge off further West. Carr describes the "encounter" as "less than inspiring," and praises the author for recognizing that both nations were guilty of crimes. Those of the Sioux are outlined in gory detail ("atrocious behavior," "sadism and blood lust," "a

particular penchant for torturing infants and children,"
etc.); the rhetoric differs for the settlers seeking *Lebensraum*
(broken treaties, hanging of 38 Sioux, expulsion even of
some who were not "guilty" of resistance, etc.) But the
difference is only fair, given the asymmetry of need in the
"encounter."[6]

The following week (March 29), we are treated to a
review by Arthur Schlesinger of John Newman's *JFK and
Vietnam*, a review by the leading Kennedy hagiographer of
a book of Kennedy hagiography. Both author and reviewer,
of course, affect a critical stance, stressing that the hero may
have erred by concealing his noble commitment to "limited
war" (wholesale international terrorism), rather than full-
scale aggression—as distinct from the lower-level aggression that JFK launched in 1961-2, another of those
unspeakable truths.[7]

Schlesinger is full of praise for Newman's "solid contribution," with its "meticulous and exhaustive examination of documents," etc.; an astonishing judgment that
merits separate discussion.[8] Newman's thesis that JFK intended to withdraw from Vietnam even without victory is
"essentially right," Schlesinger believes. He adds that he,
Schlesinger, had made the same point 30 years ago in his
chronicle of the Kennedy Adminstration, *A Thousand Days*,
where he cited JFK's view that "it was a Vietnamese war. If
we converted it into a white man's war, we would lose."

Schlesinger does not remind us that LBJ commonly
made similar remarks after picking up the mantle: We do
not want "our American boys to do the fighting for Asian
boys," he proclaimed during the 1964 election campaign.
True, this is not quite the same as the JFK-Schlesinger version: for LBJ, it was a point of principle, while for JFK-
Schlesinger, it was sheer expedience, a question of how to
win. But that aside, by Schlesinger's reasoning, LBJ must
have been deeply committed to withdrawal rather than
escalation.

Schlesinger also does not remind us that in his 940-

page virtually day-by-day history of Camelot, published in 1965 before the war had lost its popularity among elites, there is not a single phrase suggesting that JFK intended to withdraw (let alone to withdraw without victory). That striking fact leaves only three possibilities: (1) the historian was keeping it secret; (2) this close JFK confidant didn't know; (3) it wasn't true. It would be interesting to learn which of the three alternatives we are expected to choose; no hint is given, in the review or elsewhere, either by Schlesinger or those who cite him as vindicating their belief that JFK intended to withdraw from Vietnam without victory.

Both author and reviewer blame the evil military for thwarting JFK's secret designs. Both cite what Schlesinger calls "a hysterical 1962 memorandum" in which the Joint Chiefs predict "that 'the fall of South Vietnam to Communist control would mean the eventual Communist domination of all of the Southeast Asian mainland' and that most of Asia would capitulate to what the military still stubbornly called the 'Sino-Soviet Bloc'." "Such hyperbole," Schlesinger explains, "confirmed Kennedy's low opinion of the military."

Turning to *A Thousand Days*, we discover that it was JFK's *State Department* that babbled on about the "Sino-Soviet Bloc." The "hyperbole" about South Vietnam is, furthermore, standard fare in internal documents back to the 1940's, based on fear of the potential appeal of Communist success. Schlesinger also spares us JFK's thoughts on this matter. In 1956, then-Senator JFK described Vietnam as "the cornerstone of the Free World in Southeast Asia, the keystone to the arch, the finger in the dike." Burma, Thailand, the Philippines, Japan, and India "are among those whose security would be threatened if the red tide of Communism overflowed into Vietnam... Moreover, the independence of Free Vietnam is crucial to the free world in fields other than the military. Her economy is essential to the economy of all of Southeast Asia; and her political liberty is an inspiration to those seeking to obtain or maintain their liberty in all parts of Asia—and indeed the world. The fundamental tenets of this nation's foreign policy, in short, depend in considerable measure upon a strong and free Vietnamese nation"—that is, the murderous Diem dictatorship, a terror state with minimal domestic support, as generally conceded.

Perhaps JFK changed his tune later. No chance. Until the end he held that "for us to withdraw from that effort would mean a collapse not only of South Vietnam, but Southeast Asia. So we are going to stay there" (1963). Withdrawal "only makes it easy for the Communists," who would sweep over Southeast Asia; we must therefore "win the war" (Sept. 1963). Even reduction of aid to the Far East would hand Southeast Asia to the Communists and have "the inevitable effect" of threatening India and perhaps even the Middle East (March 1963). By comparison, the Chiefs sound pretty mild.

To the end, JFK's public position was that our "objective" is to ensure that "the assault from the inside, and which is manipulated from the North, is ended" (Nov. 12, 1963). The internal record hardly differs.[9] Like Newman, Schlesinger cites Michael Forrestal and Roger Hilsman as insiders on withdrawal, failing to add that Forrestal explicitly conditioned withdrawal on victory and condemned even pursuit of a "negotiated settlement...between North and South Vietnam" as "folly" (Nov. 13, 1963); while Hilsman, who (unlike Schlesinger) at least outlined the October 1963 Taylor-McNamara withdrawal proposal (partially endorsed in NSAM 263) in his 1967 book *To Move a Nation*, gave his judgment that without victory, JFK "might well have introduced United States ground forces into South Vietnam—although I believe he would not have ordered them to take over the war effort..."

To guard doctrinal purity, it is not essential to demonstrate that JFK intended to withdraw from Vietnam. Rather, it is important to ensure that debate over the US war be constrained within the dove-hawk spectrum: the permissible choices lie between international terrorism (allegedly JFK) and full-scale aggression (LBJ, the Kennedy advisers who stayed on). And all choices must be sanitized: they are defense against "the assault from the inside" in JFK's words—in fact, as he knew, the "assault" by indigenous guerrillas against a terrorist client regime that could not survive *political* competition.

If these goals are achieved, the propaganda system will have done its duty.

Sincerely,

Noam

LOOT, 3.5, May 1992

Notes

1. See Herman and Chomsky, *Manufacturing Consent*, 226f.
2. James Miller and Peter Donhowe, *Washington Post Weekly*, Feb. 17, 1986.
3. See Herman and Chomsky, *Manufacturing Consent*, chap. 5.2 and appendix 3.
4. See letter 6.
5. See letter 4, and *Deterring Democracy*, chap. 10. For a sample of Kondracke's appreciation of successful terror and his standards of loyalty to power, see *Culture of Terrorism, Necessary Illusions*.
6. Of some interest, perhaps, is Carr's response to these comments. In toto: "The notion that there have been, in American history, episodes in which *neither* side behaved like much more than bloodthirsty animals is apparently too morally complex for many to bear" (Letters, *NYT Book Review*, Aug. 23, 1992, inserted irrelevantly in an unrelated context, and without a reference to the unmentionable journal in which the comments appeared). I leave the Nazi analogue as an exercise for the reader.
7. Newman responded to what he took to be "an attack on [his] book" in *LOOT*, August; my response appears in *LOOT*, September.

8. See my article in *Z magazine*, October 1992; and my *Rethinking Camelot* (South End, 1993), for more extensive documentation and discussion.

9. Advocates of the thesis that JFK planned to withdraw without victory (including Newman) commonly allege that the internal record differs radically from what JFK said in public. For evaluation of this claim, and various related claims about high-level planning documents before and after the JFK-LBJ transition, see references of last note.

18
Rest in Peace

August 6, 1992

Dear *LOOT*,

The front page of the *New York Times Book Review*, July 23, features the headline: "You Can't Murder History"—a curious thought as we approach the anniversary of 500 years that have offered a few lessons to the contrary. We might ask, for example, how the intellectual community has dealt with the fate of the native population (as for the *Book Review*, see letter 17 for a typical example). Or the Atlantic passage and its aftermath. Or our record in Latin America, culminating in the Pol Pot-style terror of the past decade. Or the wars in Indochina. Or several other questions that might disturb tranquillity when thoughts about the murder of history are expressed in the Newspaper of Record, particularly at this historical moment.

No fear, however. The article, by Frederick Starr, keeps to a safely narrowed perspective: "History in the old Soviet Union was like cancer in the human body, an invisible presence whose existence is bravely denied but against which every conceivable weapon is mobilized." He recalls "those all-powerful Soviet officials whose job it was to suppress the public's memory" of each "grisly episode" of "the cancer of history," but who, in the end, "could not hold back the tide." Unfortunate commissars, whose power base collapsed.

The guardians of history in every society are acutely sensitive to the faults of officially-designated enemies.

The crude way to murder history is to lie. A more effective device is to set the bounds of permissible discourse. In coverage of contemporary affairs, the practice is a virtual reflex, as has been extensively documented. It is also standard in mainstream ("responsible") media critique, ensuring that unacceptable truths are banished from the mind. Thus, it is child's play to demonstrate the docility of the media with regard to US depredations in the Third World. Accordingly, the question we must ponder is whether they went too far in their anti-establishment zeal. Typical is an academic study of the media on Central America and the Middle East, which focuses on a single question: Was the anti-US, anti-Israel bias of the media utterly uncontrolled, or kept within tolerable bounds?[1] The technique requires lock-step loyalty, rarely a problem.

This method of murdering history should be part of the tool kit of any aspiring commissar; correspondingly, it is a source of endless frustration—if not amazement—for those who are seriously interested in the functioning of the ideological institutions. Suppose that it were demonstrated by the standards of *physics* that in case X, the media distorted reality in the interests of state and private power, with volumes of solid and conclusive documentation, careful and proper sampling, etc. The entire edifice can be overthrown with a flick of the wrist. The first step is to ignore the demonstration, or perhaps note it with a few derisive remarks and lies (overwhelming domination of the means of expression ensures that these will be effective, and can be endlessly repeated with impunity, even if refuted). The second is to raise the Important Question: In case X, were the media (and the intellectual community generally) too anti-American, too fierce and extreme in their denunciation of American institutions and values, or did they at least make an effort to achieve some balance, allowing a pathetic small voice to those who saw something good about America. No evidence is required to show that this is the appropriate question; it is enough to formulate it as the only question on the table, thus eliminating even the possibility that a critical thought might reach the mind. We then proceed to debate the Important Question, confident that any challenge to political correctness has been eliminated before we start.

The "propaganda model" holds that serviceability to power is a basic factor influencing the media product. If the thesis is correct, it follows that the more firmly established the conclusions of the model, the more it will be marginalized and vilified. The technique just described is the preferable one, not only achieving the desired effect but avoiding the threat that a dissident chord might be heard. This is one of the many predictions of the model that is quite well-confirmed.[2]

An enlightening example of the technique is the recent book *Battle Lines* by Jim Lederman, who has reported from Israel for National Public Radio for many years. The *Times* reviewer, Trudy Rubin, opens by noting that the book offers "some thoughtful insights" into the fundamental question: "whether American news media cover Israel impartially," or whether they are too critical and pro-Palestinian, perhaps even anti-Semitic.[3] The bounds having been properly set, there is no fear that the real world will intrude.

As a side comment, we may note that NPR is bitterly denounced as virtually a PLO front by those who describe themselves as "supporters of Israel" (more accurately, in my opinion, supporters of Israel's degeneration and ultimate destruction). We learn a good deal about these elements and their values by looking closely at what arouses their ire. That aside, as commonly observed, the major contribution to the propaganda system is made by those who stake out their position at the dissident extreme, saying in effect: Thus far, not beyond. Both of the books just cited (Bolling, Lederman) satisfy this important condition.

The media have afforded the PLO many victories, Lederman writes. One "tribute to the PLO's early media successes" is that Palestinian nationhood is "virtually unquestioned today" apart from "far right" extremists, while the US media refused to be "co-opted" into Israel's "nation-building enterprise." "Many journalists who met [Arafat] were mesmerized,…and bought [his secular democratic state] as a viable idea," though it "died a slow death" in the media. But Arafat's moderate image "has remained part of the media's vocabulary"—an absurdity, as demonstrated by the murder of Leon Klinghoffer, Lederman notes with derision (in contrast, Shimon Peres is a true moderate, unsullied by the slaughter of 75 people when he bombed Tunis a week earlier).

In the early '70s, Golda Meir tried "to entice the media...at least to carry the Israeli version of events *alongside* that of the Arabs" (his emphasis). But it was a lost cause. By 1976 Palestinians in the territories became "a focus for foreign journalists' interviews," and the US media were soon succumbing to the "Palestinian system of press co-optation." The pro-Palestinian stance came naturally to journalists who "had matured during the period of the civil rights struggle in the United States," and hence viewed Palestinians "as the Middle East equivalents of the blacks in the United States," Israel being an Alabama sheriff. By the mid-'80s, "the foreign press was standing by, waiting to report, ready to become the Palestinians' communications pipeline to the world."

Israel's efforts to gain at least some media attention had suffered a further blow in 1977, when Sadat travelled to Jerusalem, revealing an interest in peace for which Israeli officials were "totally unprepared"; they had "merely scoffed" when Lederman "told Israeli officials of my findings" after a visit to Egypt in 1974, learning "to my surprise" that Egyptians "wanted some sort of long-term political settlement with Israel." After 1977, "Israel had to compete more than ever before for newspaper space or broadcast time, for the privilege of having its positions relayed to the world by the foreign press." When the Intifada broke out in December 1987, Israel was no longer even in the competition, as the pro-Palestinian, anti-Israel passions of the media hurtled out of control.

This grim story of media bias includes some real horror stories. One of most appalling examples is the "favored technique" of ABC's Bill Blakemore, who regularly "took a classic Israeli symbol and either debunked its traditional meaning or used it to create a visual false analogy." Thus, this sly scoundrel contrasted the living conditions of the Israeli settlers in the Gaza Strip with those of the local populace in one of the most miserable and oppressed corners of the world. And he revealed that "Israel's 'redemption of the land' was predicated on the destruction of Arab villages and the dislocation of Arabs from their homes" 40 years earlier (not to speak of massacres). "One must question whether the intent was not to delegitimize the entity for which these symbols collectively stood—in this case, the State of Israel." Such journalistic dishonesty illustrates the inveterate hatred of the media for the State of Israel, and their long-standing sympathy for its oppressed victims.

We now understand why the media have so insistently proclaimed their enthusiasm for Arafat and a Palestinian state (if not a "secular democratic state," replacing Israel), focused laser-like on the denial of elementary rights to Israel's non-Jewish citizens and the racist repression in the territories, denounced Israeli terrorism while extolling Palestinian righteousness, and now revile the Bush-Baker "peace process" because it rejects the national rights of the Palestinians as a point of departure and bars their chosen representatives from participation.

Despite this somber record, Lederman urges a more nuanced view. Israel has not been entirely without resources: "Both the Israelis and the Palestinians had vocal supporters in Washington with easy access to the media [and] active media watch groups..." Furthermore, "A careful study of the nightly newscasts in the United States proves fairly conclusively that there was no universal, overt anti-Semitism or anti-Zionism in the coverage...," and Israeli charges "that some camera crews actually staged events never have been substantiated." "There is no evidence of collusion or conspiracy by the television networks." Though some journalists, notably Peter Jennings, used the TV "medium to pursue personal political agendas" (pro-Arab, anti-Israel), others, like John Kifner, were just "unprepared" (which accounts for his exposure of the truth about Beita, for example).[4] And some journalists are capable of real "insight, analysis, and nuance," particularly *Times* correspondent Thomas Friedman.

Lederman's delivery is ex cathedra, untroubled by evidence except of the kind just illustrated—a wise move, given what the facts would reveal; for example, about Friedman, whose record is particularly astonishing, as already noted.

Sometimes, a ray of light breaks through. Thus, before the Intifada, Lederman writes, journalists had "dismissed or ignored...charges of harassment or brutality by the Palestinians in the occupied territories." That is not quite true; when brutal treatment of Palestinians reached extremes, as in 1981-2, there was some media attention, occasionally at other times. But this comment is essentially correct. To learn the facts, one had to turn to the Israeli press (which Lederman falsely claims was more of an Israeli government "partner" than the US media), human rights reports, and other articles and books that were scrupulously prevented from infecting the public mind. Lederman does not indicate how this brief flash of insight conforms with the rest of the story just outlined.

Facts are not part of this game. The purpose, rather, is to shift the burden of proof, in the manner of the man who cries "Thief!, Thief!" when caught with his hands in your pocket. The nature of the task is illustrated by Lederman's tales about the peace process." The Israeli officials who "scoffed" at his 1974 revelations were fully aware that three years earlier, Sadat had proposed a full peace treaty to Israel (with nothing for the Palestinians); out of history for Lederman and his colleagues, because the US backed Israel's rejection of it, along with the January 1976 Security Council resolution already discussed (letter 1). Also murdered are the PLO initiatives in later years for negotiations with Israel leading to mutual recognition, inconsistent with US-Israeli rejectionism and therefore largely blanked out of the media. And a host of other examples, a few already noted.[5]

Keeping to the rules, Lederman offers us a "history" in which the US earnestly seeks political settlement, Palestinians insist on violence, and Israelis advocate "land for peace." This phrase Lederman identifies with "Israeli withdrawal from the occupied territories"; in reality, the phrase unequivocally refers to the Labor Party's rejectionist Allon Plan and its descendants, which leave Israel in control of the resources and useful land of the territories. The PLO, he tells us, held firm to their "rejectionist positions" and "unwillingness to compromise" or to put forth any "political agenda," insisting on "snatching all of the cake" as all other "constants in the Middle East" became reasonable, and silencing any local voice by terror. The facts—which, equally unequivocally, refute these charges—are dismissed to the proper oblivion.

The PLO bombings of Israel in 1981-2 were in part "a war of attrition against the Israelis," but even more, "a military campaign against an idea," the idea of peace. Given doctrinal requirements, it is irrelevant that it was Israel that was regularly breaking cease-fires with heavy bombing while the PLO observed them, leading finally to the Israeli invasion of Lebanon to shut down the irritating PLO pursuit of peace—as one can readily learn from mainstream Israeli sources. Lederman's account does have one merit: it reflects most US media coverage, then and since.

Lederman tells us that the media missed the real story of the Intifada. True, Palestinians threw stones at Israelis, but that was only because they were there. They were "symbols of authority"; the real target was the PLO and the traditional society. Furthermore, the PLO "strangled" the Intifada and rang its "death knell" with its violent suppression of local organizations and initiatives and "old and bankrupt" rejectionism. This war between the Palestinians and the PLO (and traditional authority generally) is the real story, missed by the media.

Every competent observer agrees that 20 years of Israeli repression and its "creeping annexation" were "what
finally sparked the Intifada" (Israeli journalist Danny Rubinstein, who has covered the territories expertly for many
years).[6] But at least in this case there is an element of truth
embedded in Lederman's constructions. The Intifada was,
indeed, a social revolution, crushed by Israeli violence that
was motivated in part by long-standing fears of secular
nationalism and moderation. The story was indeed missed
in the mainstream, though covered in the independent
media and books, another unstateable fact.[7] As for conflicts
between local elements and the PLO leadership, they are as
"surprising" as the Egyptian interest in peace, evident to
anyone who has taken the trouble to visit a Palestinian
village or town; though the same local leaders who quite
freely and openly denounce the PLO—apparently unaware
of the PLO terror that silences every independent voice—
tell you that for better or worse, it remains the political
representative of the Palestinians. The popular committees
and other local initiatives were real and important, but they
had largely been organized by the PLO and the Communist
Party, and repressed by Israel.[8] Throughout, the PLO continued to propose the "political agenda" that the US and
Israel reject and that Lederman-Friedman, et al., therefore
cannot hear, or allow others to become aware of.

To murder history, we must "mobilize every conceivable weapon" against the cancer of truth.

The true commitments of the dominant intellectual
culture, media included, are illustrated by the award to
Times columnist and former Executive Editor A.M.
Rosenthal of the Defender of Jerusalem Award for his journalistic contributions, and the response it evoked; we might
ask what the reaction would be if the PLO, or indeed any
State other than Israel had granted such an award to a
figure of comparable prominence and influence. Or by the
frank statements of its chief diplomatic correspondent,
Lederman's hero Thomas Friedman, who tells us that "For

me [Israel] is like an old flame... We're in love—there's no two ways about it"; and his call for Israel to run the occupied territories by terror and repression, in the manner of South Lebanon, though if "Ahmed has a seat in the bus, he may limit his demands" for national and human rights.[9] Or the regular odes of the editors to "this tiny nation, symbol of human decency," the kind of rhetoric rarely found apart from the annals of Stalinism. Or by the casual contempt for "Palestinians...and other Third World detritus" (columnist Joe Klein), "people who breed and bleed and advertise their misery" (Ruth Wisse, rewarded for such elegant evocations of *Der Stuermer* by a professorship at Harvard). Or by the racist diatribes against Palestinians (and Arabs generally) that disgrace the respectable press and journals, eliciting no comment.[10] Or the regular use by quite witting journalists of "experts" from the Washington Institute for Near East Policy to cloak Israeli propaganda as "objective reporting." But more significantly, by the actual practice, of which Lederman's contributions are a revealing example.

Lederman also offers a general theory of the media. "Free democratic societies" value the press "as a public watchdog..., raising issues for public debate" in a "competitive information marketplace." Americans "choose to buy their information" in "media department stores," so every niche is filled. As proof, he offers the debate over the Gulf war, when "dissenting voices" were freely heard and "a full-fledged national policy debate...carried out," ensuring that "most of the domestic political positions and points at issue had been brought to the fore for discussion before the final decision to go to war was made." "This slow, media-directed process played a critical role in unifying the vast majority of the American public around the war's aims and objectives." The miracle of the market could not be more wonderfully revealed.

We see again the utility of confident pronouncement untroubled by disruptive fact. Clearly, the basic question in the months before the US went to war was whether it should pursue the peaceful means required by international law, or resort to violence. The President had announced at once that diplomacy was excluded. Accordingly, the "media-directed process" simply suppressed the diplomatic options that had opened from mid-August 1990, lauding the President for rejecting negotiations because "there can be no reward for aggression," and barring discussion of the most crucial issue. Even the invocation of High Principle, which should have evoked ridicule from a literate teenager, was greeted with awe and acclaim. As for "the American public," by about 2-1 its "choice" was the diplomatic option (negotiated Iraqi withdrawal with "linkage") rejected by the President, hence barred by the media. One can only guess what the proportions would have been had people known that the position they advocated had been proposed by Iraq and rejected flatly by the US. The basic facts could be found in the independent media and Long Island *Newsday*, and there was occasional slippage elsewhere. But the public was effectively shielded from discordant facts or thoughts. In comparison with this episode of murder of current history, the topics that dominate critique of media performance during the Gulf war (Pentagon control, atrocity fabrication) pale into insignificance.[11]

Recall that this is the example that Lederman himself selects to demonstrate his free market theory of the media in a democratic society. History may Rest in Peace.

Sincerely,

Noam

Notes

1. Landrum Bolling, ed., *Reporters Under Fire* (Westview, 1985); for a detailed examination, see *Necessary Illusions* (*NI*), App. I.2.
2. See *NI*, App. I, 1, for discussion.
3. Lederman, *Battle Lines: the American Media and the Intifada*

(Holt, 1992). Rubin, *NYT Book Review*, March 1, 1992.

4. In April 1988, an Israeli hiker, Tirza Porat, was killed in the West Bank village of Beita, setting off hysteria in Israel and the US, and the destruction of parts of the village and severe punishment of its residents—though the Israeli army knew at once that she had been killed by the ultra-right Israeli fanatic who had led the hikers, along with other atrocities there for which he was responsible. The truth was quickly revealed by Kifner, whose professional integrity and competence are unusual in *Times* circles. Journalists stayed away, though the village (under military curfew) could easily be entered by back roads, as I discovered a few days later. See my article "Scenes from the Uprising," *Z magazine*, July 1988.

5. See sources cited in letter 1, note 4, for a detailed record, here and below.

6. Rubinstein, *The People of Nowhere* (Random House, 1991), 117.

7. See, among others, the reference of n. 4; articles in Zachary Lockman & Joel Beinin, eds., *Intifada* (MERIP-South End, 1989).

8. For serious discussion, see Joost Hiltermann, *Behind the Intifada* (Princeton, 1991).

9. *Jewish Post*, Dec. 18, 1991; see letters 16, 7.

10. For a small sample, see *NI*, 315-16.

11. See *Deterring Democracy* for review.

19

Class Struggle as Usual

January 19, 1993

Dear *LOOT*,

"Recently, the government [of Haiti] has been unusually aggressive in its defiance of sanctions," Pamela Constable reported as the new year opened. "Last week, [Prime
Minister] Bazin ordered 18 human rights monitors not to
travel outside the capital." "In a New Year's state-of-the-na-
tion speech delivered in a chandeliered hall and attended
by Haiti's elite, Bazin blasted world 'hostility' and an effort
to impose a foreign solution. 'This is a Haitian crisis and it
will be resolved by Haitians,' he vowed." Ruling General
Raoul Cedras agreed, saying "that Haiti's problems should
be resolved by Haitians, and not by 'personalist and
electoralist' politics or by 'meddling from overseas'." Bazin
also proceeded with plans for January 18 parliamentary
elections, to be held under the guns of the military in defiance of international appeals and "despite strong opposition from most political parties."[1]

Bazin was the US favorite in Haiti's first free elections
in December 1990, and remains so. When he says "resolved
by Haitians," he means *certain* Haitians, including some of
the 14 percent who voted for him, but not the 67 percent
who elected an activist priest from a poor parish, a last-min-
ute entry with no wealth, no guns, no foreign support, in
fact nothing going for him but a grass-roots popular movement of the poor: Jean-Bertrand Aristide.

Bazin's bluster and "unusually aggressive defiance of
sanctions" did not inconvenience weapons inspectors or
pose an alleged threat to US military aircraft. Rather, he has
been blocking investigation of ongoing atrocities, ensuring
that they can continue without interference. This defiance

did not call forth cruise missiles or bombing of Port-au-Prince, angry condemnations, efforts to implement the OAS embargo, or even the phone call from Washington, which, according to a Bazin adviser, is "all it would take" to send the ruling Generals back to quarters, *Times* Haiti correspondent Howard French reported. "Virtually all observers agree," French added, that little more would be necessary to call off the current reign of terror and restore the elected President.

But there will be no phone call: "Washington's deep-seated ambivalence about a leftward-tilting nationalist whose style diplomats say has sometimes been disquietingly erratic" precludes any meaningful pressure, French explains. "Despite much blood on the army's hands, United States diplomats consider it a vital counterweight to Father Aristide, whose class-struggle rhetoric...threatened or antagonized traditional power centers at home and abroad."[2]

The "counterweight" is therefore to hold total power while the "leftward tilting nationalist" remains in exile, awaiting the "eventual return" that Bill Clinton promised on the day of Bazin's military-run parliamentary elections, held in defiance of the OAS, the UN, the US, and others— and boycotted by the population.[3] Meanwhile, the "traditional power centers" in Haiti and the US will carry on with class struggle as usual, with such terror as may be needed in order for plunder to proceed unhampered. And the new enthusiasts for (highly selective) "humanitarian intervention"—cheerfully oblivious to history and such tiresome topics as the institutional roots of policy—will "forget" the possibility of such intervention as a few stern words to the killers.

Aristide was inaugurated in February 1991, and ousted in a bloody military coup on September 30. There are two versions of what happened in the interim, both agreeing that the rampant state terror of earlier years radically declined while "the flow of boat people all but dried up,"[4] and that both the terror and the flow surged with the

September coup. Note that these are purely accidental cor-
relations, given the doctrine that those in flight are "economic refugees."

One version is given by the Council on Hemispheric
Affairs in Washington. "Under Aristide," it reports, "for the
first time in the republic's tortured history, Haiti seemed to
be on the verge of tearing free from the fabric of despotism
and tyranny which had smothered all previous attempts at
democratic expression and self-determination." His victory
"represented more than a decade of civic engagement and
education on his part," spearheaded by local activists of the
Church, small grassroots-based communities, and other
popular organizations that formed the basis of the Lavalas
("flood") movement that swept him into power, "a textbook example of participatory, 'bottom-up' and democratic
political development." His government sought "the em-
powerment of the poor," a "populist model" committed to
"social and economic justice, popular political participation
and openness in all governmental affairs"—not exactly
Washington's cup of tea. Aristide's balancing of the budget
and "trimming of a bloated bureaucracy" led to a "stunning
success" that also made White House planners "extremely
uncomfortable": he secured over half a billion dollars in aid
from the international lending community, indicating "that
Haiti was slipping out of Washington's financial orbit" and
"demonstrating a degree of sovereignty in its political affairs."[5]

A different version is given by the *Times* Haiti correspondent. He reports that Aristide governed "with the aid
of fear," leaning "heavily on Lavalas, an unstructured
movement of affluent idealists and long-exiled leftists"
whose model was China's Cultural Revolution. Aristide's
power hunger led to "troubles with civil society." Furthermore, "Haitian political leaders and diplomats say, the
growing climate of vigilantism as well as increasingly strident statements by Father Aristide blaming the wealthier
classes for the poverty of the masses encouraged" the coup.[6]

"Although he retains much of the popular support that enabled him to win 67 percent of the popular vote in the country's December 1990 elections, Father Aristide was overthrown in part because of concerns among politically active people over his commitment to the Constitution, and growing fears of political and class-based violence, which many believe the President endorsed."[7]

These *New York Times* reports are news, not opinion, so we must take them to be objective truth. As explained by *New Republic* editor Andrew Sullivan, American journalism, unlike the debased counterpart elsewhere, is "a selfless and objective pursuit of the public good."[8] Q.E.D.

Portrayal of objective truth requires a refined vocabulary. Take "civil society." Note that this concept excludes the large majority of the population, which continued to support Aristide with passion and courage; but it includes "the army and the nation's tiny economic elite," as French identifies "Aristide's opponents."[9] The folks in the gold-plated Cadillacs are the "politically active people" and "Haitian political leaders," not the organizers of the grass-roots movements. That these political leaders abhor "political and class-based violence" is amply attested by their historic practice, renewed after the coup. As for the "strident statements blaming the wealthier classes for the poverty of the masses," the thought is so outlandish and absurd that it could arise only in the minds of the affluent Red Guards of Lavalas—the *Times* version of the "textbook example of participatory, 'bottom-up' and democratic political development" depicted by COHA.

Given the assault against "civil society" by the exiles dreaming of Maoist terror, we can understand why US policy shifted so radically as Aristide took office. In the past, the US had regarded state terror with a tolerant eye, happily funding it with occasional lapses when the blood flowed too openly, and applauding the worthy advance towards democracy that is a permanent feature of client regimes. But with Aristide's election, for "the first time" Washington became "deeply concerned with human rights and the rule of law in Haiti," Amy Wilentz observes. Throughout the earlier terror, "international human-rights advocates and democratic observers had begged the State Department to consider helping the democratic opposition in Haiti. But no steps were taken by the United States to strengthen anything but the executive and the military until Aristide won the presidency. Then, all of a sudden, the United States began to think about how it could help those Haitians eager to limit the powers of the executive or to replace the government constitutionally." USAID's huge "Democracy Enhancement" project was "specifically designed to fund those sectors of the Haitian political spectrum where opposition to the Aristide government could be encouraged."[10]

As the army once again imposed a reign of terror, General Cedras accused Aristide of ruling with torture, murder, and a "reign of terror." He presented OAS negotiators with "a thick, bound dossier" on Aristide's alleged crimes. A senior military source denounced Aristide's contempt for democracy; the proof is that he "never understood" that "according to the Constitution, the president of Haiti is just a nominal president," while the "real" and "effective commander" is "the commander and chief of the army."[11]

The State Department is reported to have "circulated a thick notebook filled with alleged human rights violations" under Aristide, Wilentz writes, referring presumably to the Cedras dossier, "something it had not done under the previous rulers, Duvalierists and military men," for whom aid was justified on the basis of "unsubstantiated human-rights improvements." According to journalists in Haiti, the US Ambassador called in the correspondents of the *New York Times* and *Washington Post* for a briefing on the "dossier" that the army command had compiled, perhaps with a little help from their friends.

As the flow of refugees sharply declined under Aristide, Washington suddenly found new compassion for people fleeing unbearable conditions. Under Carter, the many boat people fleeing Haitian terror and oppression received "harsh and discriminatory treatment," human rights advocates charged, and the situation became far worse under Reagan. But after the first free democratic election and the radically improved human rights climate it brought, the proportion of refugees granted asylum sharply increased. After the coup, refugees came in a huge flood, to be imprisoned in the US Guantanamo base in Cuba, or brutally returned. Asylum virtually ended. Clinton's first move was to harshen the treatment further, "temporarily" retreating from his fervent campaign pledge.

The human rights situation within Haiti received the same curious treatment. Political killings sharply declined as Aristide took over, and of those, about 2/3 were attributed to the bitterly anti-Aristide military forces. After the coup, terror quickly mounted to Duvalier levels. The press coverage reflected these changes in the familiar way. A press review by Boston Media Action found that reporting of human rights violations (relative to actual numbers) sharply increased after Aristide's election, focusing on abuses by Aristide supporters, and declined sharply after the coup: "less than a dozen deaths that might be attributed to Aristide's followers were given almost as much weight as the 1,500 or more people killed in the coup or soon after." After the coup, the focus on Aristide's alleged human rights abuses was maintained, and there was much sober commentary on his failures as a democratic leader, which make it difficult for us—with our refined values—to lend him support. Nothing new here. That pattern has been documented over and over, extensively. The intellectual culture, naturally, could not be troubled by its significance.[12]

The OAS imposed an embargo, which the US joined. The US has a certain experience with embargoes; it is, in fact, far and away the world champion, having even gained the prize of condemnation by the World Court for its illegal economic warfare. Washington is also believed to have some experience in pressuring others when it wants its rules obeyed. This case was different however: "civil society" in Haiti opposed the embargo, while the poor majority pleaded for firm enforcement. Accordingly, Washington never figured out a way to freeze the assets of "civil society" or to hinder their shopping trips to Miami and New York by cancelling visas. It was unable to detect the "lucrative use of the country in the transhipment of narcotics" by which "the military is funding its oil and other necessary imports" (Canute James), financing the necessary terror and rapacity; or to induce the Dominican army to monitor the border to impede the flow of goods that takes care of the wants of "civil society." And the phones were out of order, once again, when the time came to call friends and servants abroad to suggest that they might take note of the embargo, which therefore remained "at best, sieve-like," James adds.[13]

If this uncharacteristic impotence elicited some thoughts here about our humanitarian and democratic passions, they were not easy to detect.

Within a few weeks, the matter was academic. On February 4, 1992, the US lifted the embargo for assembly plants, "under heavy pressure from American businesses with interests in Haiti," Lee Hockstader reported in the *Washington Post*. The editors judged the decision wise: the embargo was a "fundamental political miscalculation" that "has caused great suffering, but not among the gunmen. Since it hasn't served its purpose, it is good that it is being relaxed"—not tightened so as to serve its professed purpose, as those who endure the "great suffering" are pleading. A few months later, it was noted in the small print that Washington "is apparently continuing to relax controls on goods going to Port-au-Prince from the United States," allowing export of seeds, fertilizers and pesticides. For January-October 1992, US trade with Haiti came to $265 million, according to the Department of Commerce.[14]

The *Times* worked hard to place the proper spin on the

February 4 decision. Under the headline "U.S. Plans to Sharpen Focus of Its Sanctions Against Haiti," Barbara Crossette reported that "The Bush Administration said today that it would modify its embargo against Haiti's military Government to punish anti-democratic forces and ease the plight of workers who lost jobs because of the ban on trade." The State Department would be "fine tuning" its economic sanctions, the "latest move" in Administration efforts to find "more effective ways to hasten the collapse of what the Administration calls an illegal Government in Haiti."[15] In short, the "fine tuning" punishes the anti-democratic forces who applauded it in order to benefit the workers who strenuously opposed it. Puzzling? Not to the properly educated.

The next step was to reduce the erratic extremist to a figurehead, while authority is placed in the hands of Marc Bazin, the US favorite and therefore a "moderate"—a useful category, which, in its day, has included pleasant figures from Mussolini and Hitler to Suharto and genocidal Guatemalan Generals. That result was achieved in June 1992, when Bazin was inaugurated as Prime Minister, undisturbed by a phone call.

As the year ended, Lally Weymouth instructed the incoming US President in the *Washington Post* that if he is "genuinely concerned about improving the welfare of the Haitian people," he should end the embargo, with its "dubious purpose" of restoring the elected President, and facilitate a "political settlement." Plainly such a settlement has little room for an "extremely radical anti-American priest" who "exacerbated class strife," "showed brazen intolerance," and "condoned violence and mob terror" so extreme that "with opposition leaders fearing for their lives, the Haitian army staged a coup." The solution should be based—surprise!—on the US candidate who lost overwhelmingly in the election, but who the "elected parliament...chose" as Prime Minister after the coup. "Bazin's job now is to find a political solution" and direct policy, our job is to help him, and the job of the press is to explain why this is right and just.

Fortunately, it's easy. "Bazin is an impressive man of moderate sensibility." We must therefore "delay" Aristide's return and pursue "a policy aimed at advancing the interests of the Haitian people rather than one that promotes Aristide," who lives "in style" in Washington while the people suffer; and, in their stupidity, continue to support him fervently and call for his return—perhaps to cut off his lavish life style. If "Bazin's moderation doesn't appear to pay off," there might be a "more traditional and brutal Haitian military dictatorship" than the current "moderate" one, which ignorant Haitians describe as reminiscent of the Duvalier era. If we support Bazin, Weymouth continues, there won't be any refugee problem, because contrary to the "prevailing wisdom in liberal circles," 99 percent are "economic refugees," the "man of moderate sensibility" estimates.[16]

The *Post* refrain, incidentally, is familiar: from the days of Hitler, "moderates" have been supported with the same argument. The right kind of solution is outlined further by *Post* correspondent John Goshko.[17] It would "delay indefinitely" the return to Haiti of the "radical priest with anti-American leanings" whose "strident populism led the Haitian armed forces to seize power," and would "allow Bazin or some other prime minister to govern in his place." There is a problem with Bazin. Though he is "well-known and well-regarded in the United States," unfortunately "the masses in Haiti consider him a front man for military and business interests." So perhaps someone else will have to be selected to represent the interests of "civil society."

The scale of the delay is indicated by Howard French, referring to "diplomats"—the usual euphemism for US officials: "In the past, diplomats have said the Haitian President could return only after a substantial interim period during which the country's economy was revived and all its institutions, from the army itself to the judiciary to health care and education were stabilized." That would mean a possible return of the elected President about when the famed "trickle down" effects begin to flow down, reversing their upward course. That should overcome the danger of "personalist and electoralist politics" for a few centuries, at least. Unfortunately, French adds, "Father Aristide and many of his supporters have held out for a quick return," disruptive and irresponsible as always.[18]

The right solution was put forth in February 1992, but fell through. It is now up to Clinton to implement it, amidst a chorus of approval and self-acclaim. The basic idea is indicated in paragraph 17 of a front-page story on Clinton's decision to reverse his campaign pledge and continue "forcibly returning Haitians who try to emigrate to the United States." "During his confirmation hearings for Secretary of State," Warren Christopher "expressed support for Father Aristide but stopped short of calling for his reinstatement as President. 'There is no question in my mind that because of the election, he has to be part of the solution to this,' Mr. Christopher said. 'I don't have a precise system worked out in my mind as to how he would be part of the solution, but certainly he cannot be ignored in the matter'."[19]

A ringing reaffirmation of our fabled "yearning for democracy."

Honest commentary would place all of this in the context of our unwavering opposition to freedom and human rights in Haiti for no less than 200 years, including the murderous rampage under Wilson that imposed, under Marine bayonets, the Constitution that allowed US corporations to buy up the country, and that set the stage for much that followed. As usual, we'll wait a long time for that.[20]

Sincerely,

Noam

Notes

1. Constable, *BG*, Jan. 3 1993.

2. French, *NYT*, Sept. 27, 1992.

3. Michael Tarr, Reuters, *BG*, Jan. 19; Reuters, *NYT*, Jan. 19, 1993.

4. Editorial, *NYT*, Jan 17, 1993.

5. COHA, "Sun Setting on Hopes for Haitian Democracy," Jan. 6, 1992.

6. French, *NYT*, Oct. 22, 1991.

7. *Ibid.*, Jan. 12, 1992.

8. Sullivan, review of William Shawcross, *Murdoch, NYT Book Review*, Jan. 17, 1993.

9. French, one of a series of reports in "Clinton's Headaches: A World Afflicted by Wars and Poverty," *NYT*, Jan. 15, 1993.

10. Wilentz, *Reconstruction*, vol. 1.4, 1992.

11. Linda Diebel, *Toronto Star*, Oct. 10, 1991.

12. See Chomsky and Edward Herman, *Political Economy of Human Rights* (South End, 1979), vol. II, 54f., on the Carter period; *Year 501* on later years. *Extra!*, FAIR, Jan/Feb. 1993, on BMA report.

13. James, *Financial Times*, Dec. 10, 1992.

14. *WP weekly*, Feb. 17, 10, 1992 (Hockstader, editorial); Barbara Crossette, *NYT*, May 28, 1992.

15. Crosette, *NYT*, Feb. 5, 1992.

16. Weymouth, *WP*, Dec. 18, 1992.

17. *WP*, Dec. 20, 1992.

18. French, *NYT*, Jan. 9, 1993.

19. Elaine Sciolino, *NYT*, Jan. 15, 1993.

20. On what might be found, see *Year 501*, chap. 8, and sources cited. The forceful disbanding of the Haitian parliament and the utterly fraudulent "endorsement" of the US-imposed Constitution coincided with the disbanding of the Constituent Assembly by the Bolsheviks, the event that set off the Cold War, according to George Kennan and others. For comparison of the reactions, see *Rethinking Camelot*, introduction.

Index

Some Recent Titles from AK Press

Lies of Our Times is distributed in Great Britain by AK Distribution.

About Common Courage Press

Books for an Informed Democracy

Discussing the 1990 Nicaraguan elections, Noam Chomsky points out in this volume (letter 4) that

> Three features of the election coverage are particularly striking: first, the extraordinary uniformity, which could scarcely be matched in a well-run totalitarian state; second, the hatred and contempt for democracy revealed with such stark clarity across the political spectrum; third, and most revealing of all, the utter incapacity to perceive these simple facts. Exceptions are so marginal as to be counted mere statistical error. The facts merit careful thought. They tell us a great deal about the political culture, and give a revealing insight into the dedicated assault on democracy that has been such a dramatic feature of the period that the Commissar class, quite predictably, describes as "the triumph of democracy."

Founded in 1991, the mission of Common Courage Press is to challenge the dominant political culture by publishing books for social justice on race, gender, feminism, economics, ecology, labor, and U.S. domestic and foreign policy. The Press seeks to provide analysis of problems from a range of perspectives and to aid activists and others in developing strategies for action.

You can reach us at:

Common Courage Press
P.O. Box 702
Monroe, ME 04951
207-525-0900

Send for a free catalog!